Teaching Children with Speech and Language Difficulties

Deirdre Martin

David Fulton Publishers
London

David Fulton Publishers Ltd
Ormond House, 26–27 Boswell Street, London WC1N 3JD.
www.fultonbooks.co.uk

First published in Great Britain by David Fulton Publishers 2000

British Library Cataloguing in Publication Data
A catalogue record for this book is available from the British Library.

ISBN 1–85346–585–2

Typeset by Textype Typesetters, Cambridge
Printed in Great Britain by The Cromwell Press Ltd, Trowbridge, Wilts.

Contents

Foreword

Each publication in this series of books is concerned with approaches to intervention with children with specific needs in mainstream schools. In this preface we provide a backdrop of general issues concerning special needs in mainstream schools. The government's recent Action Programme, published after considering responses to the Special Educational Needs (SEN) Green Paper, will lead to changes in practice in the future. Following consultation, there will be a revised and simplified Code of Practice in place by the school year 2000/2001. It is intended that this will make life easier.

The SEN Code of Practice (DfE 1994a), following the 1993 Education Act, provides practical guidance to LEAs and school governing bodies on their responsibilities towards pupils with SEN. Schools and LEAs were required to regard its recommendations from September 1994. The Department for Education also issued Circular 6/94 (DfE 1994b) which provided suggestions as to how schools should manage their special needs provision alongside that made by other local schools. These documents embody the twin strategies of individual pupil support and whole-school development. The Green Paper *Excellence for All* also seeks to promote the development of more sophisticated and comprehensive forms of regional and local planning (DfEE 1997).

The Code of Practice, with its staged approach to assessment supervised within each mainstream school by a teacher designated as Special Educational Needs Coordinator (SENCO), was widely welcomed.

For example, Walters (1994) argued that 'this Code of Practice builds on good practice developed over the ten years and heralds a "new deal" for children with special needs in the schools of England and Wales'. But he also reflected worries that, in the light of other developments, the process might provide an added incentive for schools to dump their 'problem children into the lap of the LEA' rather than devising strategies to improve behaviour in the school environment. Such children, he feared, were in danger of being increasingly marginalised.

Impact on teachers

While receiving a mainly positive welcome for its intentions, the *Code of Practice* (DfE 1994a) also raised some concerns about its impact on teachers who became responsible for its implementation. On the positive side the Code would raise the profile of special needs and establish a continuum of provision in mainstream schools. There was a clear specification of different types of special educational need and the Code's emphasis was on meeting them through individual programmes developed in cooperation with parents.

However, there were possible problems in meeting the challenge of establishing effective and time-efficient procedures for assessment and monitoring. Further challenges were to be found in making best use of resources and overcoming barriers to liaison with parents.

Anxieties about the Code

Following the introduction of the Code these anxieties were confirmed by a number of research studies of teachers' perceptions of the impact of the Code. The picture which emerged from these studies showed appreciation of the potential benefits of implementing the Code but widespread anxiety, based on early experience, about the practicalities of making it work.

Loxley and Bines (1995) interviewed head teachers and SENCOs about their views on emergent issues related to the complexities of introducing Individual Education Plans (IEPs), particularly in secondary schools.

Teachers feared that 'excessive proceduralism' could lead to the distribution of resources being skewed towards meeting the needs of children whose parents are best able to understand and exercise their rights, at the expense of provision for children whose parents are less assertive and confident. Teachers were most concerned about the allocation of scarce resources and the increased responsibilities of SENCOs for managing a system likely to reduce time for direct teaching of children.

School perspectives

Most schools were optimistic about their ability to implement the Code and positive about LEA guidelines and training, but there was less certainty that the Code would improve the education of pupils with SEN.

Asked to give their opinion on advantages and disadvantages of the Code, teachers cited as positive effects:

- a more structured framework,
- growing awareness of accountability,
- a higher profile for SEN issues,
- earlier identification,
- greater uniformity in practice, and
- increased parental involvement.

The disadvantages cited were:

- lack of resources and time,
- substantially increased workloads for all teachers as well as SENCOs,
- more time used for liaison and less for teaching.

(Rhodes 1996)

Four themes

A national survey commissioned by the National Union of Teachers (NUT) identified four themes:

1. broad support for the principles and establishment of the Code of Practice;
2. concern about the feasibility of its implementation, given a lack of time and resources;
3. problems in some areas related to perceived inadequacy of LEA support;
4. inadequate status and lack of recognition for the SENCO role.

(Lewis *et al.* 1996)

Another study found patchy support for SENCOs. There were wide variations in the amount of time dedicated to the role, the amount of support from head teachers and governors, involvement in decision-making, the extent of training and the degree of bureaucracy within LEAs.

SEN Register and Staged Assessment Procedures

Although its widespread adoption makes it appear to have been a national prescription, the five-stage model suggested in the Code is not a legal requirement. The Code actually states that: 'to give specific help to children who have special educational needs, schools should adopt a staged response'. (DfE 1994a, 2.20)

It goes on to indicate that some schools and LEAs may adopt different models but that, while it was not essential that there should be five stages, it was essential that there should be differentiation between the stages, aimed at matching action taken to the pupil's needs at each stage.

Five Key Stages

Nonetheless, the normal expectation is that assessment and intervention will be organised and recorded in an SEN Register for which the SENCO is responsible. The following description briefly summarises usual practice, with Stages 1–3 school-based and Stages 4 and 5 the responsibility of the LEA.

Stage 1
Class teacher identifies pupils with learning difficulty and, with support from the SENCO, attempts to meet the pupil's SEN.

Stage 2
Class teacher reports continued concern and SENCO takes responsibility for the special response to meet the pupil's SEN.

Stage 3
SENCO organises support from external agencies to help in meeting the pupil's SEN.

Stage 4
The LEA is approached by the school with a request for statutory assessment.

Stage 5
The LEA considers the need for a Statement of SEN and completes the assessment procedure; monitoring and review of the statement is organised by the LEA.

Each book in this series, explains how this process works in relation to different disabilities and difficulties as they were described in the 1981 Act and shows how individual needs can be identified and met through IEPs. While forthcoming revision of the Code may alter the details of the stages, the principles of the practices through which needs are specified will remain the same.

Information for colleagues, governors and parents

Ensuring that the school provides all necessary information for staff, governors and parents is another major element of the SENCO role. *The Organisation of Special Educational Provision* (Circular 6/94) (DfE 1994b) sets out the issues which the school should address about its SEN provision, policies and partnerships with bodies beyond the school.

This is information that must be made available and may be found in school brochures or prospectuses, in annual reports to parents and in policy documents. The ultimate responsibility for following the guidance in the Circular rests with the head teacher and governing body but the SENCO will be engaged with all these issues and the Circular forms in effect a useful checklist for monitoring the development and implementation of the SEN policy.

You may find it useful to consider the following points as a way of familiarising yourself with provision in your school.

Basic information about the school's special educational provision

- Who is responsible for coordinating the day-to-day provision of education for pupils with SEN at your school (whether or not the person is known as the SEN Coordinator)?

- Arrangements need to be made for coordinating the provision of education for pupils with SEN. Does your school's SENCO work alone or is there a coordinating or support team?
- What are the admission arrangements for pupils with SEN who do not have a statement and is there any priority for SEN admissions?
- What kind of provision does your school have for the special educational needs in which it specialises?
- What are your school's access arrangements for pupils with physical and sensory disabilities?

Information about the school's policies for the identification, assessment and provision for all pupils with SEN

- What is your school policy on allocation of money for SEN resources?
- How are pupils with SEN identified and their needs determined and reviewed? How are parents told about this?
- What does your school policy say about arrangements for providing access for pupils with SEN to a balanced and broadly-based curriculum (including the National Curriculum)?
- What does your school policy say about 'integration arrangements'? How do pupils with SEN engage in the activities of the school together with pupils who do not have special educational needs.
- How does your school demonstrate the effective implementation of its SEN policy? How does the governing body evaluate the success of the education which is provided at the school for pupils with SEN?
- What are the arrangements made by the governing body relating to the treatment of complaints from parents of pupils with SEN concerning the provision made at the school?
- What are your school's 'time targets' for response to complaints?

Information about the school's staffing policies and partnership with bodies beyond the school

- What is your school's policy on continuing in-service professional training for staff in relation to special educational needs?
- What are your school's arrangements regarding the use of teachers and facilities from outside the school, including links with support services for special educational needs?
- What is the role played by the parents of pupils with SEN? Is there a 'close working, relationship'?
- Do you have any links with other schools, including special schools, and is there provision made for the transition of pupils with SEN between schools or between the school and the next stage of life or education?

- How well does 'liaison and information exchange' work in your school, e.g. links with health services, social services and educational welfare services and any voluntary organisations which work on behalf of children with SEN?

In any school those arrangements which are generally available to meet children's learning needs will have an impact on those services which are required to meet specific needs. It is therefore very important that a reader of any one of this series of specialist books makes reference to the general situation in their school when thinking about ways of improving the learning situation for pupils.

Harry Daniels and Colin Smith
University of Birmingham
February 1999

Bibliography

Crowther, D., Dyson, A. *et al.* (1997) *Implemention of the Code of Practice: The Role of the Special Educational Needs Coordinator.* Special Needs Research Centre, Department of Education, University of Newcastle upon Tyne.

Department for Education (DfE) (1994a) *Code of Practice on the Identification and Assessment of Special Educational Needs.* London:HMSO.

Department for Education (DfE) (1994b) *The Organisation of Special Educational Provision.* Circular 6/94. London: HMSO.

Department for Education and Employment (DfEE) (1997) *Excellence for All: Meeting Special Educational Needs.* London: HMSO.

Hornby, G. (1995) 'The Code of Practice: boon or burden', *British Journal of Special Education* **22**(3) 116–119

Lewis, A., Neill, S. R. St J. and Campbell, R. J. (1996) *The Implementation of the Code of Practice in Primary and Secondary School: A National Survey of the Perceptions of Special Educational Needs Coordinators.* The University of Warwick.

Loxley, A. and Bines, H. (1995) 'Implementing the Code of Practice: professional responses', *Support for Learning* **10**(4) 185–189.

Rhodes, L. W. (1996) 'Code of Practice: first impressions', *Special!* Spring 1996.

Walters, B. (1994) *Management of Special Needs.* London: Cassell.

CHAPTER 1

Introduction

This book is written particularly for newly qualified teachers who have not worked in mainstream classrooms with learners who have speech and language difficulties. Experienced teachers may also find it helpful if they are new to working with learners who have these difficulties. The ideas in the book are set in the inclusive context of a mainstream classroom, where children with different language learning needs are supported to access a broad and balanced curriculum. Inclusion is not only a geographical phenomenon, and teachers need to be supported in developing professional knowledge, understanding and skills in order to facilitate all children in the UK accessing a broad and balanced curriculum, wherever they are at school. Teachers in specialist provision may also find this book helpful.

The book aims to develop teachers' knowledge and understanding about learners with speech and language difficulties and to offer skills and strategies for supporting this group of learners to access the curriculum. It also develops teachers' knowledge and understanding about working with parents and other professionals in education and in health who are involved with learners who have speech and language difficulties.

Teachers who have not worked with children with speech and language difficulties before have said that they need a 'language to talk about language and language difficulties'. This book explores ways of describing and talking about language. Sharing a 'language to talk about language and language difficulties' enables teachers to talk with other teachers and professionals about children who have speech and language difficulties. It is valuable for several purposes:

- it is a way into the jargon words and phrases used by other practitioners in the field;
- it is a way of understanding how practitioners in related fields think and talk about the subject and the difficulties;
- it can help to heighten learners' and teachers' awareness, and recognition, of areas of difficulty;
- it can enable teachers and other practitioners, such as speech and language therapists, psychologists, learning support assistants and Special Educational Needs Coordinators (SENCOs), to share a common language for discussion of children's needs.

When teachers and other practitioners share 'a language to talk about language' they can develop mutual understanding, appreciation of differing perspectives and collaborative work around language. Teachers are also in a position to talk about language with learners and to discuss explicitly the nature of speech and language, their difficulties and the strategies which will support them.

A final aim of the book is that, having been introduced to the field of learners who have speech and language difficulties, teachers and other professionals and parents can promote and support the development and implementation of a whole-school approach towards the inclusion of these learners into the wider curriculum and learning environment of the school. They may also be encouraged to study and explore more in this area.

Language variation

There is a wide range of regional variations of English. We pronounce words differently often depending on where we live: how we say mug, bath or court, use words differently (donny/hand, canny/clever) and put words together differently.

The so-called standard form of speaking, such as the BBC news readers, where there is reduced or no regional variation, is called RP (Received Pronunciation). Written English is less affected by regional variations. There is a standard form of written English which is taught in school and used officially. From time to time difficulties in understanding arise between speakers of different regional variations, but these are not the focus of this book.

Developmental variation

Most children and young people as they grow up show difficulties in speech, language and communication. For example, many three- and four-year-olds pass through a brief period of stammering, many children pronounce words incorrectly, particularly words that they have just come across, many chose the wrong word because it sounds similar to the one they need (e.g. interview/interval), many will start and re-start sentences and correct themselves. Many will misunderstand what is said to them, mishear what is said to them, and also not 'do as they are told'. As peers and adults we accept all of these variations as part of growing up and developing language skills.

However, we become alert to some children and young people who show variations in understanding language and in expressing themselves because they are noticeably different from their peers. In many cases these variations result in breakdown in communication between the child and the person they are talking with. These variations are often perceived as difficulties because they persist and challenge the communication skills of the person who tries to communicate with the child or young person. Yet with appropriate strategies on the part of *both* parties, most children and young people with speech, language and communication difficulties can communicate effectively. This book aims to identify these difficulties and some appropriate approaches and strategies which can help learners in understanding and using language effectively.

Language as a secondary difficulty

There is a wider group of learners who may have difficulties developing speech, language and communication skills because their main (primary) difficulty is in a related area of learning, such as hearing impairment, physical impairment, more generalised cognitive and learning difficulties, emotional, social and behavioural difficulties, and those whose difficulties are on the autistic spectrum.

EAL learners

Sometimes, learners of English as an Additional Language (EAL) are included with children and young people who have difficulties with language and communication. Often many of the same approaches and strategies for understanding and using language can be used to develop the English language of this group of learners. The important point to bear in mind is that EAL learners are usually competent users of other languages. They do not have difficulties understanding or using their other (home, first) language. They need help to develop English for immediate learning purposes and usually in the context of the curriculum.

Some EAL learners may have specific language and learning difficulties and the teacher needs to be alert to this possibility. It is important that teachers observe and record the learning of each EAL learner and differentiate the curriculum so that language learning and cognitive learning can be distinguished. Other aspects need to be distinguished such as the pace and style of learning of the EAL learner which may indicate other learning needs. Newly qualified teachers and teachers who are new to teaching EAL pupils need to be in touch with colleagues who are experienced in special needs and/or EAL teaching in order to understand and meet the diverse and complex needs of EAL learners with additional special educational needs. There are some helpful books in this area:

Hall, D. (1995) *Assessing the Needs of Bilingual Pupils: Living in Two Languages*, London: David Fulton Publishers.
Gravelle, M. (1996) *Supporting Bilingual Learners in Schools*. Stoke: Trentham Books.

Children with primary difficulties in speech and language

Children who have speech and language difficulties come from all socio-economic backgrounds. Three times as many boys as girls have communication difficulties. Delay in developing speech and language can be due to intermittent hearing loss or lack of stimulation in early life. More persistent speech and language difficulties may be linked to genetic factors, brain damage at birth, and syndromes, while for a great many the cause remains unknown (I CAN 1999).

Estimating the exact figure for the number of children with speech and language difficulties is hard, partly because studies have given this group of difficulties different labels, such as developmental aphasia, auditory agnosia, specific language impairment, language delay. Recently, figures have been obtained for children who have a primary difficulty with speech and language and referred to as having a **specific speech and language difficulty (SSLD)** (Dockrell and Lindsay 1998). In the United States, prevalence is estimated as 1:10 of school-aged children , while a recent study in Cambridgeshire reported that just under 7 per cent of three-year-olds have language difficulties. However, many children, about 40 per cent with language delay in the preschool period, catch up in their language development during the early school years. Yet, the majority (about 60 per cent) who had preschool language difficulties, continue to have language difficulties at ten years of age, and are likely to have them through secondary education and adulthood. In many cases the language difficulty may evolve and change, or the pupil may develop additional difficulties such as with social or literacy skills.

Translating these figures into likely numbers of children with speech and language difficulties in inclusive classrooms, I CAN (1999) suggests that there may be 1:8 children in nurseries, and 1:5 entering school with noticeable speech and language difficulties, which may drop slightly in junior and secondary classes. In junior and secondary classes with between 30 to 40 pupils, there may be about eight learners with speech and language difficulties.

Of concern is that a recent study showed that there are children in mainstream classes with language difficulties who have not been identified and may not be receiving the support services they need. They depend on the professional development of their teachers to identify, assess and support their speech and language needs for curriculum learning. Furthermore, while a high number of children are recognised as having literacy difficulties, their difficulties in vocabulary and grammatical comprehension are not noticed (Dockrell and Lindsay 1998).

Further reading

You can read about this study in an article by Julie Dockrell and Geoff Lindsay, called 'The ways in which speech and language difficulties impact on children's access to the curriculum', published in 1998 in *Child Language Teaching and Therapy*, Volume 14, Issue 2. The prevalence figures were cited from this article.

Conclusion

This book aims to raise teachers' awareness, knowledge, skills and understanding about pupils in their mainstream classes who have a range of speech, language and literacy difficulties. At the end of this book you should be able to identify, informally evaluate and implement support strategies with pupils who have a communication difficulties.

CHAPTER 2

Understanding speech and language

Language is a broad category which includes receptive language (understanding) and expressive language across different components: speech sounds, words, sentences, meaning and use of language. Speech is a particular component of language and children can have speech difficulties alone or in combination with difficulties in other components. This chapter looks at the different components and requirements for developing speech and language and at different analogies for language which help us understand it better.

Prerequisites for developing speech and language

Certain prerequisites contribute to the development of speech and language. A primary prerequisite is that children must want to communicate; without this *motivation* it is difficult for them to develop meaningful language. Healthy *development of the brain* and structures involved in speech, such as the mouth, are essential. *Cognitive skills* such as memory, attention and listening are very important. *Short-term memory* is needed in processing speech input and passing information to *long-term memory* where it is laid down as representations and schemas, to be retrieved later. *Attention skills* are important to prepare the system to be in a state of readiness for listening. *Listening* is noticing meaningful sounds (auditory perception) and discriminating between appropriate and inappropriate information and between similar sounding words (auditory discrimination). *Hearing* is important for the development of typical speech but hearing loss does not prevent the development of language. Alternative forms, such as signing, can develop. Finally, an important prerequisite for language is children's *ability to symbolise* and represent reality through their own perspective, which is shown in pretend play with toys, and later in their drawing. Damage or disturbance in the development of prerequisites usually precipitates speech and language difficulties. Encouraging the development of these skills is always beneficial for speech and language development (Law 2000a).

Comprehension

Understanding spoken or written language is called *verbal comprehension*. Children from birth start to understand spoken language: their mother's voice, their own name. It is difficult to estimate how much language children understand because comprehension is difficult to measure, but it is usually more developed than expressive language. Children who have expressive language difficulties also often have comprehension delay and difficulties which may be overlooked. Problems understanding language are often associated with difficulties in cognitive skills, such as difficulties in auditory processing and understanding fast-flowing speech, or they may have difficulties sequencing and recalling what they hear. Children with verbal comprehension difficulties often rely on their *non-verbal comprehension* skills. They understand the non-spoken clues in the context of language, such as pointing and looking at what we are talking about, laughing, facial expressions, and other people's reactions to spoken language. Children can have difficulties understanding different components of language: discriminating between sounds, understanding different meanings of the same word, understanding different types of sentence structure, and understanding a paragraph of written text.

Expressive language

Children usually develop the components of expressive language in parallel. Delay or unusual development in one or more components usually effects all aspects of language to a greater or lesser extent, although often only the area showing the most difficulty receives support.

Vocabulary

Children who have difficulties learning new words are likely to have more pervasive language and communication difficulties.

Vocabulary is described in two main categories of words: **function** and **content** words. Function words are a small group of words used for grammatical purposes, such as pronouns (e.g. she, they, we), prepositions (e.g. in, on, between, behind) and conjunctions (e.g. and, but, because, since). The larger group, content words, includes all the other words referring to our knowledge of the world. Function words usually have only one main meaning with some variations depending on context while content words have many meanings, and are entirely defined by the context in which they appear.

Many words can have different roles in sentences, for example, 'elderly':

 (i) The elderly man had fought in the war
(ii) The elderly are living longer

In (i) 'elderly' functions as an adjective and in (ii) it is a noun. This kind of example is frequently found in school textbooks. Children with language learning difficulties are often confused by these changes of role, and change in the grammatical role of words needs to be pointed out and carefully explained. In their expressive language, children with language difficulties may learn to avoid these situations and use a strategy of 'one word = one role', particularly in their writing, which may be restricting.

Content words

Children learn to develop content vocabulary by learning to 'label' aspects of their environment, people, objects, experiences and events. They develop a range of meanings and 'package' them into one word, and they relate meanings of words to build up 'networks' of words and meanings. There are four important ways in which words 'network':

- sameness (synonyms)
- oppositeness (antonyms)
- categories (hyponyms)
- subcategories (subordinates).

To understand the meaning of a new word, we go through a process of finding words it networks with: means the same as, different from, words it would be categorised and subcategorised with. The following quote from a teacher illustrates how word meaning is built up from networking the meanings of other words:

'Who is the president of the United States? You see America doesn't have a king.'

The 'United States' and 'America' are used here as synonyms, while 'president' and 'king' do not have exactly the same meaning, although they belong to the category of 'constitutional leaders'. The second sentence supports the meaning of the first. This is an example of language which teachers and others use most of the time when they talk to young children and learners in class because it is an important strategy for teaching and conceptual development.

Concepts are also closely linked to **semantic fields**, grouping words which belong to the same category, such as animals, buildings, transport, people at work, entertainment. Grouping related words by semantic field lends itself to curriculum work, such as specialised subject vocabulary and topic work.

Vocabulary has a system with rules which determine the organisation of meaning and words. Words are not free-floating, or learnt in isolation. They are linked and related and their meanings are shaped by the meaning of other words in context.

Multiple meanings

Most words have more than one meaning. Confusion is usually avoided because speaker and listener choose the same, most appropriate meaning for the word from the context, that is the topic being talked about and the words which surround it. Most children develop multiple meanings for words if they are introduced to them. However, children with difficulties in learning words and meanings may only have one meaning for a word and they fail to understand additional meanings in what has been said, or what they have read. For example, the boy who was told that his pregnant sister had gone into labour, thought she had joined the Labour Party.

Children with difficulties learning word meanings are helped by identifying or being offered synonyms and opposites for the new key word. This is an important technique in teaching children with these difficulties and can form part of a pre-teaching vocabulary session.

Grammatical role and meaning: Word meanings can change with different grammatical roles. For example, 'light' has 31 different meanings and uses (Sinclair 1987) which vary depending on whether 'light' is a noun, verb, or adjective. Children with difficulties in this area need explicit teaching of the different meanings when they occur. Children who have linguistically deprived backgrounds will need to be exposed to the range of meanings, although they are likely to learn them more quickly.

Literal and abstract meanings: There are a range of other meanings of 'light' which are more abstract and often form part of stock expressions, or idioms. For example, 'a light in her eyes', 'to see the light', 'to throw light on the matter', 'a light at the end of the tunnel', 'in the light of new information', 'to see things in a different light'. Children in upper junior and lower secondary school enjoy teasing apart the literal meaning from the more abstract in these sayings and turns of phrase. However, children with difficulties in learning words and word meanings will find this a difficult, and in some cases, an impossible, exercise. They benefit from clear links being made between the literal meaning of the word and its more abstract usage. In the example of 'light', the basic meaning of 'light' – 'the thing that lets you see things' – has to be related and interpreted to the abstract usages for children with language difficulties through explicit teaching and discussion.

Grammar (syntax)

'Grammar is the rules of a language, concerning the way in which you can put words together in order to make sentences' (Sinclair 1987). Poor vocabulary development is often associated with difficulties developing grammar (Lock 1993). To develop sentences children need to have a certain amount of vocabulary items which include the necessary elements to make up an utterance. Their vocabulary needs to include content words, such as nouns, verbs, prepositions, and adjectives, across a range of topics so that they can form meaningful strings of words. They also need to develop function words to support grammatical sentences.

Function words

Function words are sometimes called 'the little words' in sentences. In fact, they are a small group of words used for grammatical purposes. Unlike content words they usually have only one meaning. Some may have no meaning at all, serving only to make grammatical sense. For example, what is the meaning of: 'do', 'am', ' to' or 'the' in sentences like these?

  (i)   Do you want to go to the party?
 (ii)   I am happy.
(iii)   They are walking to the park.

In (i) 'do' has no meaning but it is needed to make the question form. In (ii) 'am' has little meaning although it shows that the time is 'now'; the meaning would not change if you said: 'me happy'. If (iii) were said as: 'They walking park', the meaning would be largely intact. Developmentally, children leave out function words like 'do', making question sentences with intonation patterns, and saying 'me happy'. We tend not to correct young children's grammar, but are more interested in the truth value and accuracy of what they are saying (Brown 1973).

There are children, though, who as they grow older continue to have difficulties using function words and developing grammatical forms. As in the example of 'me happy', they seem to speak like a telegram, i.e. telegraphically. They say only the key information words, omitting the function words, and this also shows in their written work.

Supporting children who have grammatical difficulties can be approached through their strengths in understanding meaning. It enables them to develop cognitive strategies based on meaning and sense. For those who are writing, work with model sentences, such as through worksheets, can be helpful strategies to support the grammatical aspects of language difficulties. With children who have grammatical difficulties it is important to work closely with speech and language therapists, who can identify the grammatical structures and function words which the children need to develop. They can be built into curriculum work through the children's individual targets and plans.

Morphology

Content words also have their own grammatical structure which is usually shown by suffixes and prefixes (**morphology**) which can add grammatical information and also change the word class of the original word. For example, nouns have plural endings (bus/buses), verbs have endings (walk/walks/walking/walked), adjectives can change to adverbs by adding -*ly* (soft/softly). Children usually acquire this kind of word grammar early on (about two years) in their language development. However, children who have difficulties with grammatical structure find them hard to learn. Although much time and energy is spent teaching grammatical word endings to children with language difficulties, many continue to have difficulties beyond school.

Other grammatical changes to words can extend or negate the original meaning of the word. For example, putting *un-* as a prefix makes the word mean the opposite (happy/unhappy), similarly with *dis-* (able/disable). There are also suffixes, such as *-ness*, which changes the word class of adjectives to nouns (kind/kindness), and *-able*, which changes nouns to adjectives (knowledge/knowledgeable).

Upper junior and lower secondary pupils are usually taught these aspects of morphology in the curriculum. However, children with grammatical language difficulties need more examples, repetition, and time to learn the rules behind these word changes. Careful planning of necessary vocabulary and clear explanation of the rules for the word changes support successful learning by children with difficulties in this aspect of language. However, irregular word changes, such as 'noble/ignoble' can cause confusion and may never be learnt successfully by this group of children.

Development of grammar

Most children develop the skills and rules to make well-structured meaningful sentences by the time they are three-years-old. They continue to develop their grammatical skills by developing more complex structures, such as sentences with two or more clauses, such as 'if . . . then . . .', to express more complicated ideas until about ten years of age. Grammatical development continues in written language (Perera 1986). Children develop increasingly complex sentence structures in their writing, partly because they have come across them in reading and partly because they are thinking more complex thoughts. Far from completing grammatical development at three or five years of age when they seem proficient, children continue to develop grammatical structures throughout secondary school, and beyond.

Children who have difficulties with grammatical structure usually show specific difficulties when they are about three-years-old, in comparison with their peers. They have difficulties with word order, function words, making longer sentences (a string of four words or more) and as they grow older difficulties expressing complex thoughts because they lack the structures for combining words into meaningful sequences. Even though their speech sounds may be clearly articulated they are difficult to understand because of the telegraphic quality of their utterances. As they grow older the detail that is left out in their telegram-like utterances makes it increasingly difficult to understand them. Some children become frustrated at not being understood and develop behaviour difficulties, such as temper tantrums and aggressive behaviour towards the listener and others who fail to understand them. Unfortunately, the aggressive behaviour may gain adult attention and subsequent referral for support, leaving the underlying primary language difficulty unnoticed.

Using language – pragmatics

The skills which we use to interact effectively, share meaning and communicate with each other are known as **pragmatics**. Communicating is not just about using the appropriate sounds, words and sentence structure because it goes beyond these skills. As a listener, to interact effectively means interpreting what the speaker is meaning to say and reading between the lines of the more obvious structural properties of language. As a speaker, it means that we imply more than we say and we infer more meaning than is actually said (Law 2000a). We use language for a purpose (function) and in a context. Some purposes are:

- forms of politeness: 'Could you open the window?' means 'open the window'

- jokes and humour: What do you get when you cross a kangaroo and a sheep? A woolly jumper (two meanings of 'jumper')
- sarcasm: 'I am glad to see you have graced us with your company' to a pupil who arrives very late for class means the teacher is not glad but angry about the pupil's late arrival
- wit and irony: 'He's a good catch' means one thing if you are talking about a wicket-keeper and something else if referring to your friend's partner
- close-friends-talk: talk about personal concerns which would not be spoken about with others.

Context

There are several different aspects to contexts which children need to develop communication skills for, and in which some children and young people can show difficulties communicating. Here are a variety of contexts in which we can observe children and young people demonstrate pragmatic skills (Anderson-Wood and Smith 1997).

Situation: people communicate better in certain situations than others, such as at home better than at school.

Activity: it is easier to communicate about activities we are doing now, than to recall and talk about activities we did yesterday or some time ago.

Role: we need to be aware of the roles we have in the interaction, e.g. communicating between equals requires different skills from communicating with authority figures.

Relationship: we communicate differently with people who are strangers from those we know, and that relationship effects the interaction.

Current relationships: we interact differently with those we are friends with from those we have just had a quarrel with.

Knowledge of partner: the state of knowledge and emotional state of people influence how and what we talk to them about.

Topic: what we have to talk about influences the quality of our interaction, whether we know a great deal and whether we can be imaginative.

Linguistic context: what has just been said influences how we interact, depending on our understanding and our grammatical, lexical and phonological skills.

Inferential context: understanding beyond the literal meanings of the words and sentence structures influences our understanding and the appropriateness of our interaction.

Unlike other components of language, there are no rules which govern pragmatic skills. They vary across societies and between cultural groups and even within cultural groups, and between boys and girls. Learning pragmatic skills has as much to do with social skills as it does with language skills. Children who have difficulties with pragmatic skills show difficulties in both these areas.

Most young children learn to develop pragmatic skills from babyhood, but there is a small group of children who have substantial difficulties and have to be taught how to 'read the signs' for successful social interaction. The signs include contextual clues, non-verbal cues, different meanings to words, and appropriateness.

Non-verbal communication

Even when we are not talking we are communicating. There is a range of non-verbal signals which we use to communicate with, either on their own or to support what we are saying, e.g. eye contact, pointing, gestures and mime, body language, facial expressions, moving the person to, or fetching what is wanted. Children with difficulties in this area may use non-verbal signals in an unusual way, while children with receptive language difficulties may rely on them.

Eye contact is a basic requirement for successful interaction. Pupils with speech and language difficulties often learn to look away and not to make eye contact with the person who is speaking or listening to them. This is likely to be interpreted negatively by adults. For children with language difficulties it is often an expression of embarrassment and inadequacy. Encouraging and maintaining eye contact during communication with these pupils is very important.

Motivation to communicate

Most children want to talk and communicate with others. They may prefer to talk with particular people in their environment more than others. They may even prefer not to talk at certain times, in certain places and to particular people. They will have topics which motivate them to talk more than others. Teachers are interested in identifying topics which excite children and motivate them to talk and communicate. Children who do not talk are usually noticed by parents, family, friends and teachers, and their silence or sporadic communication may be due to various reasons, usually involving social and psychological factors.

Low self-esteem

Children with substantial expressive language difficulties are motivated to communicate, even though it is a frustrating experience. It is usually psychological factors which make them stop communicating. If they may become depressed by their lack of success at talking and remain silent, preferring not to talk, then they need to be referred to a speech and language therapist. Self-confidence through successful communication strategies is fundamental to motivate them to communicate. For some children with substantial difficulties, strategies may include communication boards, flash cards and a signing system. They may also need counselling about coping with their speech and language difficulties.

Selective mutism

Some children choose when and where they wish to speak and in other places they will not speak. For example, they may speak at home but not at school, they may speak to one friend and to no-one else. They are selectively mute. However, they still communicate to others, non-verbally, as well as through writing and drawing.

Autism

Some children with severe social and psychological difficulties and with autistic spectrum difficulties may have limited motivation to socially interact with others, and to communicate with them. They seem to live in a world of their own and need a great deal of planned intervention and therapy to develop aspects of communication.

Conversation

The most common context for talking is conversation, and there are several characteristics which children learn about conversing: to take turns, to introduce, maintain and switch topics, to request and make clarifications when they do not understand, and to listen. They also learn not to behave in other ways if they are to be successful conversationalists, such as interrupt, talk for too long or too loudly about things their listener is not interested in. They learn that conversing is about cooperating through language.

Language is used for a variety of purposes, such as to ask questions (obtain information), direct others, pretend and imagine, point out, recall, argue and deny. The balance between these purposes varies according to the activity we are engaged in, for example, free play, versus a cooking activity. In interactions we expect the person we are interacting with to maintain and complete the exchange in an appropriate way, and we make allowances for different interpretations of what is said. Taking account of personal and external contexts is essential in assessing the appropriateness of children's and young people's pragmatic skills. However, we notice children who have unusual interactions and difficulties conversing because they do not follow the implicit rules of conversation and have difficulty maintaining the topic.

Classroom talk

The most frequent shape to classroom talk is one mainly controlled by the teacher, who initiates (I), the pupil responds (R), the teacher may reinforce (R), and gives evaluative feedback (F); the so-called I-R-(R)-F. In most classroom talk two-thirds of the turns are taken by the teacher (Hughes and Westgate 1998). The pupils are limited to a response-level interaction within a learning frame which is determined by the teacher. In small groups, teachers have the opportunity to explore interactions which are teacher-led rather than teacher-dominated. Teacher-led interactions which use supportive talk strategies 'enable' children to be more interpretative and speculative (hypothesising) in their language and thought.

Rather than only asking factual-recall questions, offering more 'communicative space' in the dialogue, allows children to be challenged linguistically and mentally through sensitive teacher-guided discourse (Hughes and Westgate 1998). Practitioners in classrooms who are not teachers, such as classroom assistants and nursery nurses, often show more skills in doing this (Hughes and Westgate 1997).

This approach is more successful with children who have difficulties maintaining interactions. Controlled dialogues often do not allow much speech processing time, requiring quick responses, and few opportunities for child-led dialogue topics, which are easier for this group of children to maintain.

Speech

Speech is a motor skill, as well as a mode of language expression, and it has two levels. *Articulation* is a particular kind of motor skills learning where moving our speech articulators in rapid, precise and coordinated sequences becomes automatic.

Phonology, on the other hand, is the system with rules to organise speech sounds into sequences to make words. Phonological knowledge informs us that changing a speech sound in a word, changes its meaning: pat/mat; pat/pot; pat/pal.

There is a 'loop' so that we hear and monitor our speech and can change it to produce the target phonological word.

It is important to discern when children have difficulties in speech: the extent to which they are due to articulation difficulties, i.e. motor skills, and the degree to which they are phonological difficulties, i.e. difficulties with linking speech sound changes to meaning.

Part of the process of making speech sound sequences automatic is that the phonological system lays down a 'representation' of the speech sound sequence, at a cognitive level of language functioning. Children can refer to this **phonological representation** when they are becoming aware of the different speech sounds in a word. They learn to map the speech sounds to written forms, letter–sound correspondence, at the beginning of learning to read.

Speech sounds, that is, consonants and vowels, are the **segments** of the word. There are 44 speech sounds in English which contrast with each other to make words.
Speech sounds and writing: Speech sounds in English have alphabetic representations but it is not always one-to-one. For example, the following words are all pronounced the same way but spelt differently: sense, scents, cents; hire, higher, and possibly, hiya. When listening to children speak, we need to train our ears to listen to the speech sounds rather than thinking of the written form of the word.
Voicing qualities, or **prosody**, refers to other other features of speech which are meaningful. Intonation patterns, i.e. the musicality of an utterance, and pitch changes indicate questions, exclamations, humour and emotion. Rhythm (i.e. beat) and fluency maintain a flow which facilitates listeners' understanding and difficulties with fluency result in stammering. Changes in prosodic features draw

attention to and emphasise the important meanings of the utterance. Difficulties in prosody are often shown in children who have difficulties using language (pragmatics).

Syllables are the basic unit for speech. In English, the most common syllable is consonant, vowel and consonant (CVC): mum, cup, dog, knife, house, but syllables may also be CV, VC, and CCVCC (plant) and longer words are poly-syllabic. The opening consonant(s) of a syllable is the *onset*, the vowel is the *nucleus* and the final consonant(s) is the *coda*. The nucleus and coda are the *rime*. Many teachers are familiar with this analysis through phonological approaches to reading and spelling. Syllables carry the beat – strong and weak – of the word, so that 'balloon', has a weak first syllable and a strong second syllable. The beat of the syllables in words helps to set a rhythm for the whole sentence and utterance, and helps to draw attention to the important meanings.

When we learn new words we pay attention to the onset and the syllabic beat. It is helpful to explicitly draw attention to these two features when teaching new vocabulary to children with speech and language difficulties.

Development of the phonological (speech sound) system

Children do not develop each sound, one at a time. They develop their speech sound system through a series of phonological processes, based on rules which effect the sounds and syllables in words and which make their early words easy to say. For example, one child's development of the words 'story' and 'stream' show the development of sounds through *phonological processes* from about two to four years of age:

dohdi – dohli – stohli – stohri (story)

deem – dleem – stleem – streem (stream).

Box 2.1: Examples of phonological processes

Phonological processes **Some examples:**	
delete weak syllables:	balloon – 'boon'
delete coda:	fish – 'fi'
use the same consonant sound throughout word:	butterfly – 'tutati'
make 'back-of-the-mouth' sounds at the front of the mouth:	car – 'tar'
reduce clusters of consonants to one consonant:	star – 'tar'
Phonological processes can occur together: e.g. *guitar*	
fronting of back sounds:	guitar – 'titar'
+ weak syllable deletion	'titar' – 'tar'

The examples in Box 2.1 show that the child may have three different meanings for one of their words: 'tar' refers to car, star and guitar. Speech like this would quickly become unintelligible to the listener, who would have to rely on the context to understand what the child was talking about.

Interestingly, children rarely respond to direct correction of their speech. Changing pronunciation patterns needs to be approached through the child's phonological system. Consider this example of a father with his four-year-old son:

Child: mahmade peez
Dad: Do you want the marmalade?
Child: ye
Dad: say marmalade then
Child: mahmade
Dad: no, marmalade
Child: mahmade
Dad: look, say mah
Child: mah
Dad: mal
Child: mal
Dad: ade
Child: ade
Dad: right, marmalade
Child: mahmade

The difference between the father's and the child's pronunciation is that the child is not saying the second syllable because he is using the rule which deletes weakly stressed syllables in words. He needs, first, to become aware of the weak as well as the strong syllables, and then the beat of the syllables in any word. The father here soon became exasperated, and felt that his son was teasing him; then he thought he was being stubborn and the boy became dejected. These feelings are not unusual, and to avoid them it is important that new vocabulary is introduced from several angles; meaning, syllables, speech sounds and grammatical function. In an older child, perhaps over five or six years of age, difficulties with polysyllabic words may be linked with sequential memory difficulties and a speech and language therapist's advice should be sought.

Box 2.2 shows the pattern which most children follow in establishing their speech sounds in first language English.

This kind of information is helpful because it gives a broad indication of typical development which allows teachers and others to identify children who are developing in a different way and alerts us to monitoring their speech sound development. Children who arrive in Nursery and Reception classes with unintelligible speech should be referred to the speech and language therapy service.

Children at about three to four years of age may show interruptions in **fluency**, by hesitating and repeating words or part of words. This is usually a phase which passes as children's language matures. Disruptions in fluency at this young age are best managed by drawing no attention to them at all, allowing children to focus on 'what' they are saying rather than 'how' they are saying it. However, if disruptions in fluency persist until six or seven years or older, the child needs to be referred to a speech and language therapist for **stammering**.

Box 2.2: Typical pattern of speech sound development (from Law et al., eds, 2000b, page 18)

Speech sound development

Age at which 90 per cent of children have acquired the sound and vowels:

3 years	m b p h w
4 years	k g t d n ng f
5 years	s z l v y th sh ch
6 years	r j

Intelligibility to strangers

2 years	25%
2.5 years	60%
3 years	70%
4 years	90%

Grammatical role of some speech sounds

Some speech sounds also carry grammatical meaning. For example, consider the role of the sounds 's', 'z', 't' and 'd' in these word endings:

plurals:	cot – cots, pram – prams
possession:	girl's, children's
she/he/it:	walks, runs
past tense:	walked, called

Children with speech difficulties can also have difficulties with grammar.

Analogies for speech and language

One way of understanding something is to think about it through analogies and metaphors. There are several analogies for understanding speech and language. These are discussed here.

Language is like a tree

James Law suggest that language is like a tree (Law 2000a). The metaphor of the tree is able to show some of the important characteristics about language as well as the important relationships between its components. Language is like a tree because:

- they are both dynamic, growing and changing;
- they are both systems which are rule-governed;
- they both are made up of different components;
- they both have visible, measurable parts and hidden parts;
- they both need to interact with the environment in order to grow.

Law develops the analogy by making comparisons between the components (see Box 2.3).

Box 2.3: The language-tree analogy and language (Adapted from Law *et al.*, eds, 2000b)

Roots	Factors contributing to communicative development: motivation to communicate brain development hearing cognitive skills: memory: short-term and long-term attention listening: perception and discrimination ability to symbolise: pretend play
Trunk	Comprehension: verbal non-verbal
Branches	Vocabulary Grammar: morphology sentence structures
Leaves	Speech: articulation phonology voice fluency prosody

Language is like the tube map

Another good analogy for processing information in the brain is the London tube map. Language is like the tube map because it shows:

- a system of communication;
- information travelling in both directions;
- where lines of communication meet at certain points;
- that the underlying 'processing' map does not resemble the surface map.

The strength of this analogy is that it shows language as a system, with information flowing through it, and where the relationship between surface and underlying structures is not straightforward.

Language is like a container

A third analogy is the 'container' metaphor for language, which presents the image that language development is like a container which can be 'filled up' as language increases. A development on this is the 'bucket' analogy. A bucket with holes in it and water seeping out, is like a child with language difficulties. Language cannot develop to its full potential because of the difficulties (Crystal 1987). The disadvantage with this analogy is that it envisages language as a static and simple entity.

The tree analogy is much richer and more accurate in helping us to understand language. It captures the idea of different components interrelated in a complex system which is growing and changing in response to the environment.

Conclusion

This chapter has looked at the language system, by describing its different component systems, aspects of their development and ways in which the components relate to each other. Areas of difficulty in the components have been pointed out and this is taken up more fully in the next chapter. One of the most effective analogies for understanding the language system and its interrelated components is the tree.

CHAPTER 3

Understanding speech and language difficulties

The last chapter looked at ways in which language can be described. This knowledge is applied in this chapter to the way in which we describe and understand the difficulties which some children and young people have in developing speech, language and communication. Other descriptions and explanations for these difficulties are also presented. At the end of the chapter you should be aware of the four important approaches to understanding speech and language difficulties, the nature and range of difficulties there are and the terms and labels used to describe these difficulties.

What is in a name?

There are a range of labels which are used when talking about and describing speech and language needs of some learners. For example, they can be described as having 'difficulties', 'delay', 'deviance' or 'disorders'. Often these terms come from different professional groups and different sources of knowledge and study. There are instances when terms and labels are not shared by professionals and parents and when the same terms are used to mean different things. These cases can lead to confusion and frustration for those involved. Terminology 'messiness' reflects the deeper situation that there is a great deal that we are still not clear about in the field of speech, language and communication difficulties. This section tries to clarify some of the general terms used in disability, and a later section 'A medical approach' discusses more specific labels used for speech and language difficulties.

Delay is often used to describe some aspects of language development of a child which, when we compare them to peer language, seems to be more like that of a slightly younger child. Further, we may continue to monitor the child's development and find that those aspects of language development 'catch up' and the child speaks and communicates like the rest of the group. With hindsight, we can say that the child's language and communication was following a recognised path but was 'delayed'.

Deviance is usually used to describe a child's language development which does not 'catch up' and persists in being atypical in some or all aspects of speech and communication. For example, there are some children whose language and communication seem to be so delayed that we may be concerned that they will not be able to catch up with the peer group's: such as children who have not started talking by three or four years of age, or who only use single words to express themselves at five years of age. The language development of these children is not following a typical pattern. It seems to be 'deviating' from the recognised developmental path.

Disorder is often taken to mean the same as 'deviance', and usually indicates a complex and persistent language and communication difficulty. It is most frequently used by those who have a medical-model approach to special educational needs, although teachers and other educationists also use it. Some educationists prefer not to use this term because it emphasises a medical base to the child's or young person's communication difficulty.

Impairment indicates that the language and communication system is not functioning to its 'normal' capacity and is impaired. Impairment emphasises the damaged or limited resources in the individual in a particular area, such as hearing impairment, visual impairment, speech impairment.

Disability is the term often preferred by most people who have, or who are carers of those who have, substantial, complex and long-term difficulties in speech, language and communication. The term 'disability' has a social perspective. When other people and the environment change and accommodate the person's disability, the person becomes 'enabled'. By the same token, when we do not accommodate, we can further disable the person with difficulties. For example, the mobility of people in wheelchairs is enhanced when there are ramps beside stairs. Children and young people with speech and language difficulties and disabilities can communicate more effectively in supportive and enabling communicative environments.

Difficulties is a more generic term which can embrace all the other terms. It is more likely to be used by educationists because it suggests there is challenge which can be overcome. It is also used to mean that the challenge needs to be met with strategies from *both* parties in the communication process.

Summary

The above discussion makes several points. Firstly, there is no single way of describing the complexity and persistent nature of speech and communication difficulties. Terms have their own histories and groups who prefer to use them. Secondly, there is very little scientific justification for preferring to use one over another. These terms are descriptive and do not indicate a difference in the nature of the communication difficulty. Even the term 'delay' which indicates the short-term nature of the difficulty is only justified with hindsight. Thirdly, many of the terms emphasise the 'abnormality', 'wrongness' and the negative aspects of differences in development of the child's speech and language. Finally, they highlight the individual aspect of the difficulty, that the 'problem' lies in the child and young person rather than emphasising that the interaction between individuals can be enabling or disabling.

Teachers and others who work with children and young people who have speech and language difficulties need to consider the terms which they prefer to use, since these terms reflect how they think about and approach their work with this group of learners. Despite the variety, parents and most professionals prefer to use terms and labels in identifying, and trying to understand, children's and young people's speech and language difficulties.

Approaches to understanding language difficulties

There are four important ways in which professionals and parents understand speech, language difficulties and needs which children and young people have: medical, linguistic, psycholinguistic, educational. These approaches, like the terms discussed above, are based on professional preferences and a range of bodies of knowledge.

A medical approach

Understanding speech and language difficulties from a medical perspective means looking for medical, biological or neurological causes and 'cures' for the difficulties. Medical causes of persistent specific speech and language difficulties (SSLDs) are thought to be due to brain damage, particularly at birth, genetic factors or related to syndromes (I CAN 1999). Other medical conditions, such as epilepsy, can give rise to severe speech and language difficulties. Accidents and illnesses in childhood can result in similar difficulties. However, there are many children with speech and language difficulties for which there is no known cause. Many labels for speech and language difficulties come from a medical approach.

Speech

Physical disability can cause speech difficulties, effecting the learning of motor skills for speech. This group of speech difficulties is called **dysarthria**. Related difficulties may occur with swallowing (**dysphagia**), chewing, mouth and lip closure (resulting in drooling), voicing and breathing.

Physical disability, such as cerebral palsy (CP), can be caused by brain damage, resulting in muscles being too tight, too floppy, or difficulties with coordination. The physical difficulties range from mild to severe and often physiotherapy and speech and language therapy are needed. Cleft lip and palate are abnormalities of the structure of the mouth and face which effect speech, and can be caused by genetic factors, as well as drugs and viruses during early pregnancy, such as flu and rubella. When successfully operated on in childhood there are few speech difficulties.

Genetic factors can also cause difficulties which effect learning and possibly language, such as Down's Syndrome.

Some *progressive disabilities*, such as muscular dystrophy, or brain tumours, can bring about dysarthria and a gradual deterioration in speech and eating skills.

Some types of medical intervention can be effective at improving speech, such as drugs, and exercises, such as breathing, swallowing and 'articulation' exercises.

Voice

Difficulties with producing voice are called **dysphonia**. There may be no voice, or the voice quality is rough, hoarse or croaky. In children dysphonia can be caused by abnormalities of the structure of the larynx, accidents which paralyse one or both vocal cords, and genetic factors, in some syndromes.

More usually though, they are caused by environmental factors, such as voice strain due to excessive shouting, e.g. while playing. The 'cure' is to stop abusing the voice by shouting. Teachers often suffer from vocal strain and in severe cases, vocal abuse, in teaching. The 'cure' is voice rest and changing the stressful way the voice is used. Pupils and teachers with recurring or persistent voice problems should be referred to the speech and language therapist.

In secondary schools, some teenage boys' voices do not 'break', and they continue to have child-like high pitched voices (puberphonia). This may cause them embarrassment and they may be teased. Referral to a speech and language therapist as soon as possible is recommended. Puberphonia can be caused by physiological and/or psychological factors and drug therapy and/or speech and language therapy are usually successful.

Stammering

Stammering (or stuttering) is a difficulty with the fluency of speech. Everyone's speech is slightly dysfluent with some hesitancies and repetitions, particularly when we are nervous. Stammering becomes a difficulty when **dysfluency** upsets communication. Stammering has several characteristics: hesitations, repetitions of words and parts of words, as well pauses and in severe cases blocking – an inability to say the word. Some children, often the very bright, control their stammer by talking around a word they feel they might stammer on (circumlocution) and the listener is impressed by their talkativeness and vocabulary range. Young children of about three to four years of age often show a dysfluency in their speech, which is usually a developmental phase which they pass through after a few months. It is best to draw no attention to this. Stammering in older children is usually due to a complex web of emotional, social and psychological factors. Children should be referred to a speech and language therapist as soon as possible and advice sought from the therapist about classroom support. It is best not to make demands for public speaking on learners who stammer unless they perform well. Stammering can also provoke teasing from peers.

Language

A medical approach labels language difficulties as 'disorders' and identifies three main subtypes: receptive/expressive language disorders, expressive disorders, and higher order processing disorders.

The most severe language difficulty children can have is when they cannot make sense of any auditory input, particularly not speech sounds and appear 'word blind'. This is **Verbal Auditory Agnosia** (VAA), or *severe receptive/expressive deficit syndrome*, which can be due to genetic factors or an acquired epilepsy syndrome, and is associated with autism. It is extremely difficult to assess these children's hearing, and they may appear to be functionally deaf. They are usually non-verbal and can be taught to communicate through visual channels, such as signing, communication boards, reading and computers.

There is a case study of a four-year-old child with this difficulty who was identified in a nursery class: Martin, D. and Reilly, O., (1995) 'Global language delay: analysis of a severe central auditory processing deficit', in M. Perkins and S. Howard (eds) *Case Studies in Clinical Linguistics*, London: Whurr.

Developmental dysphasia refers to specific language difficulties in receptive and expressive language in children from the outset of their language development. The cause is usually unknown but it is likely to be due to genetic factors (Rapin 1996). It first described language loss in adults, following a 'stroke' or head injury. In children, dysphasia more accurately describes language loss (i.e. acquired language difficulties) after an accident. Contrary to previous thinking, children who have acquired language difficulties do not make a full language recovery but continue to have persistent language difficulties, which may be mild or moderate. Dysphasia is an old-fashioned term and not used much now to label children's developmental language difficulties. Recent medical labels use linguistic terms, such as *receptive/expressive phonological/syntactic deficit syndrome*. Children with this severe language difficulty have most difficulty making sense of words and sentences and as a result their expressive language is very delayed.

The most common of language difficulties is the *phonological/syntactic deficit disorder*. Children with this 'disorder' have receptive language abilities better than expressive skills. They have substantial difficulties making sentences, developing speech sounds and learning new words.

Children with **verbal dyspraxia** speak little and effortfully, in short utterances with difficulties organising longer words or sentences, and a distorted and inconsistent speech sound system. It is likely to have a genetic cause, which effects neurological programming, and often forms part of a wider syndrome called Developmental Coordination Disorder. Children show difficulties with co-ordination, organisation and sequencing in many areas of their behaviour (Portwood 1999). Dyspraxia is a term which is often used and misunderstood across professional disciplines and with parents.

Language difficulties also include written forms, and **dyslexia** is a difficulty with reading, and/or spelling and usually writing. Previously it was thought to be due to visual and neurological difficulties, however, more recently, other non-medical, cognitive explanations are preferred. Dyslexia frequently occurs with children who have speech and language difficulties. It is a persistent difficulty despite conventional literacy teaching, intelligence and opportunity.

Hearing impairment nearly always effects speech and language. Hearing can be impaired centrally, that is in the brain and auditory nerve, in the middle ear (between the ear drum and cochlea), and the outer ear. Central, or sensory, impairment results in more profound hearing loss and is caused by many factors, such as genetic factors, viruses in pregnancy, e.g. rubella, as well as childhood illnesses and accidents. Successful operations for cochlea implants can result in good language development. Hearing aids also support speech and language development. The language of deafened preschool children after a few years can become indistinguishable from that of children born deaf (Rapin 1996). Much more common in classrooms are children with fluctuating and intermittent hearing loss, which effects the development of speech and language, as well as learning, and caused by frequent colds, and ear infections. Children with frequent heavy colds who have difficulties attending in class, should have their hearing tested.

Behavioural difficulties are strongly associated with speech and language difficulties. The reasons for this are not clear. On the one hand, the frustration of not being able to communicate satisfactorily may trigger aggressive and violent behaviour. On the other hand, behaviour disorders with a medical basis, such as Attention Deficit Hyperactivity Disorders, have been found to co-occur frequently with speech and language difficulties in young children (Thorley 2000).

Children with **psychiatric disorders** frequently have associated speech and language difficulties, such as the early onset of schizophrenia, selective mutism, and autistic spectrum disorders (Baumgaertel 2000).

Autistic spectrum disorders effect cognitive, social and language development. They are due to a range of factors, including genetic, atypical structure of the brain and atypical biological and chemical functioning of the brain. There is no 'test' for autism and different patterns of behaviour produce a spectrum of autistic-type disorders. Abilities in language vary hugely across this group. Some children are non-verbal, some may echo what is said without initiating, and others may have severe difficulties understanding spoken and written language, although their expressive language is clear and well-formed. Some children and young people have a high level of language but noticeably inappropriate social use of language, and they may have **Aspergers syndrome**.

The effect of **social and environmental factors**, such as poverty, on language development is controversial, despite a great deal of research. The argument has centred on whether 'deprived' children have 'deficient' language or 'different' language. Deficient language would need intervention, while 'different' language would mean that children had the appropriate linguistic forms but not necessarily the cultural features which are often in language assessments. Verbal enrichment programmes in nursery classes are aimed at improving the language skills of this group of children.

Implications for teachers

A medical approach to understanding many aspects of special educational needs is common in certain areas of education. This approach may also be supported by speech and language therapists who work in the health service. Teachers who are concerned about a learner's language development need to find out about the pupil's hearing assessments. Children who have medically-based difficulties are often on the more severe end of the spectrum of difficulties and may require medical attention which takes them out of school a great deal, with consequences for their school work. Despite being one of the oldest approaches to understanding speech and language difficulties, the medical approach is quite limited in helping to minimise complex and long-standing communicative difficulties. The classroom teacher may need to look elsewhere for a more helpful approach for education.

A linguistic approach

Another approach to understanding speech and language difficulties is through language. A model which is often used shows three major aspects of language interrelated in a Venn diagram (see Box 3.1).

Box 3.1: The relationship of Content, Form and Use in language (Bloom and Lahey, eds, 1978)

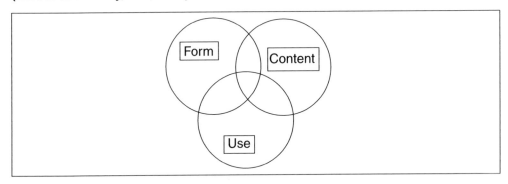

Form refers to the structures of language: grammar, morphology and phonology and it gives the shape and form to meaning, and language use.

Content refers to the meaning of language, and includes vocabulary. It links language with conceptual development as well as to Form and using language.

Use means how we use language, both for a purpose (function) and in a context, and it is like pragmatics. Meaning directs the purpose of why we speak to others and the Form of language helps us to understand and to respond appropriately in the context.

This model serves to understand language development and also language difficulties. Difficulties in Form, Content and Use can be identified in receptive and expressive language.

Difficulties in Form

Children who have difficulties with Form show delay or persistent difficulties in developing the rules and structures for grammar, morphology and phonology. Their speech is unintelligible or difficult to understand, and their utterances may be short, with key information words only, and telegraphic. A smaller group of children also have difficulties in understanding particular grammatical forms. For example, they understand:

> *the cow kissed the horse* (active)
> but not:
> *the horse was kissed by the cow* (passive)

Children with difficulties in form may have phonological or syntactic difficulties, or both phonological/syntactic difficulties. They may also have receptive grammatical Form difficulties, which is usually reflected in a lack of expressive Form, that is, short, three or four key word, utterances. This is a receptive/expressive language difficulty.

Many of the terms used in the linguistic approach to describe speech and language difficulties have also been adopted by the medical approach. However, a linguistic approach analyses the child's speech and language in order to understand the linguistic nature of the difficulty, and is not concerned with the medical or biological cause. Often the cause is unknown.

Difficulties with Content

Children who have difficulties with vocabulary, such as learning new words, understanding abstract meanings, relating words and meaning to conceptual development, and also with relations across words in an utterance, have difficulties in the Content area of language. They would also have difficulties understanding word meaning and sentence meaning, as well as concepts. They have word finding difficulties.

Difficulties with Use

Children who have difficulties using language show inappropriate interactions, often because of lack of understanding of the context, and what has been said. They may also show difficulties in the purpose and function of their own expressive language, and either not talk or talk excessively, or say inappropriate or unexpected things. Their difficulties lie in the area of pragmatics.

In describing language difficulties, sometimes the areas where the difficulties are noticed are used to describe the difficulty. For example, a *phonological* difficulty, a *phonological-syntactic* difficulty or a *semantic-pragmatic* difficulty. However, there are many other cases where children's difficulties cannot be described within one component of language. For example, when difficulties with meaning impact on sentence structure, and when difficulties with phonology effect learning new vocabulary. Children with substantial language difficulties may have pervasive difficulties across components.

Implications for teachers

Using a language approach, teachers and speech and language therapists need to work collaboratively in order to develop a 'language to talk about language difficulties'. A strength of this approach is its focus on the nature of the speech and language of children's difficulties, and in particular the quality of the interaction and communication between the learner and themselves. It is crucial for the teacher to appraise that the language in the interaction is at an appropriate level for the learner. Was the adult's language too simple or too complicated, with its implications for the learner's learning? This approach to understanding the learner's language raises awareness about modifying our own language to support understanding and maximise expression for the learner.

A psycholinguistic approach

Speech and language difficulties can be understood by looking at children's language processing abilities. There is a close relationship between learning and language. Although they are different, they share many common cognitive functions, such as attention and memory, as well as sensory skills, such as auditory and visual perception, discrimination and sequencing skills. Educational psychologists and speech and language therapists are particularly interested in this approach to understanding communicative difficulties. (It is also referred to as the cognitive-neuropsychological approach.) It opens up a way of understanding the common ground between language and learning, with ways of closely assessing skills which show the learner's strengths and weaknesses, and implications for focused intervention programmes.

The psycholinguistic approach focuses on children's abilities to receive language input, to store it, retrieve and manipulate it and then output it, in spoken and written forms. Language input is speech sounds, words, sentences, and they are stored as representations of speech sounds and words, which children can retrieve and recast for their own communicative purposes before outputting them.

Children's language difficulties can be explained by identifying difficulties in particular processing skills, such as listening skills. Listening skills include auditory perception (understanding what you hear), auditory discrimination (noticing meaningful differences in what you hear) and auditory sequencing (understanding sequences of words, instructions or a story). It is similar for visual skills.

Difficulties with auditory perception can vary from being very severe, as in verbal auditory agnosia or central auditory processing difficulties, to having difficulties understanding fast-flowing questions/answers and discussion in class.

Many children with these difficulties need time to process what has been said to them or what they have read.

Auditory discrimination difficulties can also be linked with segmentation and sequencing difficulties, e.g. discriminating between similar sounding words, *desk/decks*. Motor programming for saying words may also be affected, and children may appear to have a phonological difficulty. This may explain aspects of verbal dyspraxia. Storing and retrieving phonological and lexical representations is crucial for learning to read and spell. Difficulties at this level of processing may explain aspects of dyslexia.

This approach allows investigation at different levels to identify where the breakdown in processing is which may be responsible for the language difficulty, as well as identifying strengths in processing to be used in intervention. Children have difficulties at different levels and to varying degrees.

Implications for teachers

The implications for this approach are mainly seen in terms of assessment of skills and developing related, focused intervention programmes to build on the learner's strengths and develop weaker skills in order to improve language difficulties. While these tasks may largely be the remit of psychologists, speech and language therapists and specialist teachers, class teachers and parents are involved in implementing and supporting intervention programmes. Collaborative discussion is crucial.

An educational approach

Those taking an educational approach to understanding speech and language difficulties bring together information from the other approaches, and select relevant information which is most important to supporting children's learning. Choosing and using the information for supporting learning needs to take account of the perspectives of the child and teacher/parent, and the context for communicating.

In this approach, speech and language difficulties are understood through awareness of the discrepancy between language expectations and language abilities. For example, questions or reading tasks show and exacerbate children's speech and language difficulties when they are presented in ways and at levels out of line with their abilities.

In the same way other contexts reveal, support or exacerbate children's speech and language abilities. Important contexts for children are school, home, and other out of school situations, such as clubs, play and entertainment situations. These contexts make similar and different demands on the communication of the child and young person: social purposes, emotional and interpersonal relationships, control and regulation, and information as well as the language demands of the curriculum, such as special vocabulary, particular question–answer routines, and reading and writing formats.

An educational approach seeks to understand children's speech and language difficulties in the context of each individual child by interpreting the information about each child. The information can be applied to enhance their personal and group communication and learning.

Furthermore, an educational approach offers a link between language and learning. Language difficulties can affect difficulties in higher order learning skills, such as difficulties in categorising information, and thinking skills. Thinking skills include abilities to analyse information (break it down into constituent parts), synthesise information (reassemble the information in a new, meaningful way) and evaluate information (appraise its importance).

Teachers need to be aware of the language demands made by the aspects of the curriculum they are teaching and work out ways to support learners with communicative difficulties accessing curriculum learning. They need to be aware of the curriculum demands for the learner to express her/himself and find ways to support the pupil possibly through speech, or through alternative means of expression, such as signing. An educational approach to exploring learners' speech, language and communicative difficulties offers teachers, parents and others a way to support language and learning in a variety of contexts.

Conclusion

These four approaches are all necessary for understanding speech and language difficulties. They serve different purposes. Some try to offer explanations for causes to the difficulties, such as the medical and psycholinguistic approaches; others focus more on describing and giving a clearer picture of the difficulties. They all offer ways of intervening and maximising the communication of the child and young person with communicative difficulties. Each offers insights on particular difficulties and practitioners may prefer the approach which offers most insight for them in their work. There is great deal that teachers, parents and other professionals can discuss about their approaches to understanding speech and language difficulties as part of working together.

The educational approach underpins the discussion in Chapters 4 and 5, because it is most relevant to classroom teachers working with pupils with speech and language difficulties.

CHAPTER 4

Assessment in the classroom

One of the most important roles that classroom teachers have is their contribution to assessing the learner's communication difficulty in a range of contexts. Contributions include, for example, offering evidence about children communicating spontaneously with adults and peers, about learning, the 'here and now', past and future, fact and fiction, asking for information, following instructions. Teachers can offer information and insight on the different modes of language, speaking, listening, reading and writing used by children. The information can cover the different components of language as well as how the learner uses language for learning. This chapter looks at the procedures which class teachers can use to collect information about the speech and language of pupils whose communication is causing concern.

Screening and assessment

Purposes

There may be several reasons which motivate the teacher to gather information about the speech, language and communication of a particular pupil. For example the pupil may be causing concern because she/he is not achieving, the teacher may have difficulties communicating with her/him, the teacher may have been asked to collect information to contribute to preparing a statement of special education needs for the pupil, the speech and language therapist may have asked for the information. It is important to know the purpose for collecting the information, whether it is for your own purposes or for someone else's, whether it is for an overview or in-depth assessment. The information needs to meet the purposes. It is unlikely that the teacher will make a 'diagnosis' of the learner's difficulty on the basis of the information collected, but the information will contribute to a fuller and more accurate description of the learner's difficulties.

Procedures

There are a range of procedures for collecting information about speech, language and communication which teachers draw on, such as observation, curriculum-based assessments, reading tests, collecting background information and information from important others. We consider procedures which are useful for the whole class as well for individual pupils who are causing concern.

Identifying a group with special needs in speech, language and communication skills

It is helpful to teachers to identify early on in teaching a class, which pupils have good communication skills, who have some difficulties and who have substantial communication difficulties. This information will influence and support teachers' later decisions about achievement expectations, planning and arranging individual and group work, and planning for differentiation.

Some of the ideas in this section are based on the work by Ann Locke and Maggie Beech, 1991, *Teaching Talking: a Screening and Intervention Programme for Children with Speech and Language Difficulties*, Windsor: NFER-Nelson. The pack comprises two handbooks, for Teaching Procedures and Teaching Resources, and is aimed at pupils in nursery and junior education.

At the beginning of the school year, it is recommended to find time in the first month or half term to regularly observe the class during the teaching and learning activities the teacher has with them, as well as, if possible, other situations such as in games, in the playground, at lunchtime. It is very helpful if another adult who works with this class, for example, the classroom assistant, or EAL teacher, can also be involved in the observations. It is advisable to draw up an observation checklist which can be completed by both adults, which shows a range of communicative behaviours along one axis, and a list of each pupil in the class along the other axis. An example is provided in Appendix 1.

Charts and grids like the one in Appendix 1 can be used to record behaviours several times during the school year, e.g. each term, and yield important information in a variety of areas:

- developmental information;
- rate and pace of progress over the school year (11 months);
- areas of specific skill or difficulty;
- consistency in skills and difficulties;
- comparative information between pupils (**inter**personal);
- comparative information within each pupil's progress (**intra**personal).

The teaching staff working with this class can draw a number of conclusions. They can identify three groups of pupils based on their communication skills. For example, there would be a group of pupils who use speech and language fluently with confidence. A second group can demonstrate fluent communicative behaviour in some situations with some people but not in all situations and not about all topics, and they show some difficulties. A third group of pupils would be identified by their consistent lack or low level of communication in most situations and difficulties in listening and attending. Teachers will be able to obtain further information about identifying groups of learners based on reading, writing, spelling and pre-literacy skills.

This information will support teachers in planning differentiated learning for the three groups of pupils. It will allow progress to be logged about learners who move across groups. It also allows teachers to identify specific pupils with substantial speech, language and literacy difficulties and to plan for them both in terms of a group and as individuals. Recording communication behaviour on the same chart over the course of the school year shows which children will progress from the third group into the second and possibly first groups. Those children who do not progress will need further, more in-depth study. This information is important to pass on to the children's teachers in the subsequent year group, as well as to the SENCO.

Focus on individual children

Individual children who are giving particular cause for concern in their speech and language development should be referred for a hearing test and to the speech and language therapist. Teachers may like to seat the child nearer to them, although children can misinterpret this, to facilitate more and better communication with the child. Background information about a pupil who may be causing concern should be available in the child's school file. Information about development, previous assessments, support and progress are also usually kept there. When the child is new to the school this information may not be available.

Important others

Talking with the SENCO about pupils giving rise for concern is essential. Initially, the discussion may be simply to voice your concerns about some pupils' communication skills and difficulties. The SENCO may be able to advise about the kind of information which would be particularly important as well as possible approaches for collecting the information. Talking with the child's previous teacher where feasible, whether in the school or by phone, about your concerns will also be helpful.

There are important others who may be contacted later when you have some clearer ideas about what your concerns are. Visiting the child's parents to discuss your concerns can be helpful but may be deferred for a while, otherwise the visit may result in alarming the parents and raising anxiety unnecessarily. You may want to have developed some specific questions about the child before contacting the psychologist and speech and language therapist.

Information from formal testing procedures

Formal tests which class teachers are likely to use to throw light on language and communication difficulties will be to do with reading, writing and spelling. Other formal tests for speech sounds, vocabulary, grammar, and cognitive tasks for auditory and visual skills are likely to be carried out by the SENCO, the learning support teacher, the psychologist and the speech and language therapist.

There are often logistical problems in arranging to carry out a test procedure, such as finding time and a quiet place to carry out reading tests in the classroom. Futhermore, the teacher needs to be familiar with administering the test before carrying it out with a pupil with difficulties.

The relevance of doing tests for reading, writing and spelling depend on teachers' abilities to interpret the pupil's performance on the test items in terms of the her/his general, everyday language and communication skills, and to use them to inform teaching and intervention programmes. The teacher does not need to do this alone, but together with others interested in the child or young person. Discussion beforehand, about the key features which the teacher needs to note, may help. For example, reading fluently and accurately but without understanding, demonstrated by not being able to answer questions about the text. This is sometimes called 'barking at print', or **hyperlexia**.

For young children, in preschool and infants, teachers may be interested in exploring the development of conceptual skills. Tests, such as the Boehm Concept Test (Boehm 1986), give insightful and helpful information about children's understanding of concept words, for example for place, position, and time.

Difficulties in learning mathematics are frequently connected to difficulties in understanding the language (Grauberg 1999). There are procedures which explore concepts used in mathematics such as the Early Mathematics Diagnostic Kit (Lumb and Lumb 1987) which shows a child's understanding of, for example, ordinal numbers, comparison of length, and sequencing.

The important point about these procedures is that they try to identify the concepts which the child has and where the language for the concept may be helping or hindering learning. This information will contribute to the teacher's perceptions of the child. Teachers can take into account the child's level of understanding in these areas, and they can adapt and make more understandable their own language when talking to the child as well as plan to develop the child's understanding through teaching.

Informal procedures

Informal procedures for assessing the speech, language and communication skills of pupils with needs in this area include checklists, and interviews with parents. The most familiar checklist used by teachers is the AFASIC Checklist (see Appendix 2). It is developed by AFASIC (Association For All Speech Impaired Children) which is a support organisation for children, young people and their families who have communication difficulties. There are checklists for infant and junior aged children which collect information on aspects of the development of speech and language, such as speech sounds, vocabulary and sentences. It is a simple and efficient way to identify which aspect of the child's language is causing concern. The information can be useful in seeking support from the speech and language therapist who can take assessment further.

When a pupil raises the teacher's concern because of lack of communication, not speaking, using gestures, or appearing withdrawn, then the teacher may want to ask the parents or care-givers about the child's or young person's communication at home and out of school. *The Pragmatics Profile of Everyday Communication Skills in School Aged Children* (Dewart and Summers 1995) is a set of interview questions which ask the parents or care-givers about how the child or young person communicates with them in specific situations. For example, when she/he wants something that is out of reach or when she/he wants to go somewhere else, how does she/he communicate her/his needs. The information can help the teacher understand the communication repertoire of the pupil which could influence how she/he interacts with the pupil.

Parents may want to complete the Profile at home when they have time to think about the questions and the way their child communicates. Information from the Profile can be compared with information from colleagues about the pupil's communication. A wider Profile of the pupil's communication inside and outside school and in a variety of contexts with a range of people can be drawn up. This information can contribute to knowing the pupil better, and understanding the role which each person has, teachers and parents, in maximising the effectiveness of the child's or young person's daily interactions.

Summary

The approaches to assessment discussed here offer a 'snapshot' of the child's language at a particular moment. They are valuable but they do not contain the child's spontaneous communication and could even be artificial. The following approaches try to capture and describe the natural, 'live' language of the learner, which is an essential companion to information from more contrived situations.

More detailed assessment approaches

More detailed information about communication behaviour, gathered from observing the child and young person allows us to *interrogate their behaviour* more closely. That is, we have the opportunity to look for and notice interesting things that the child does which we might not understand or too quickly reach a conclusion about. We also have the chance of analysing these observations and finding patterns where there seemed to be only meaningless behaviour.

Observation

There are three common ways of observing pupils' speech, language and communication in the classroom: the diary method, an observation chart, and audio tape recording.

The diary is an exercise book where you jot down particular utterances which the pupil makes and the context of the interaction. You can carry the 'diary' around with you to be able to jot down immediately what is said. You may also want to add your own comments about your first thoughts on the observation. See the example in Box 4.1.

Box 4.1: Diary entry of observation

I hand J. back his history exercise book with his marked homework in it.

On opening book he sees my comment and reads it aloud to no-one in particular: 'See me'. J. looks up and again to no-one in particular says: 'see me? see me? How can I see me?'. Puts book down and gets on with previous work.

Comment: At first, I thought that J. was being silly, then I realised that he just didn't understand what my comment meant. He understood 'me' referred to him as the reader, not to 'me' who was the writer. Literally, of course, he couldn't see himself! He might have thought this was a bizarre comment at the end of his homework! These utterances I overheard have made me realise that J. is most probably not understanding a lot of what is said to him when the language moves away from the literal and requires any sort of reflexive thinking, and where he is not doing the action. I'll look out for more of these examples. How could I write 'see me' another way?

This example illustrates that one good observation of a person's behaviour is worth more than some results from contrived tests, in offering an insight into how learners with communication difficulties use language. Weighed against the enormous value of these kind of observations is the considerable time they take to write and to comment on. However, if you decide to note down only those events which you recollect easily then diary observations become more manageable. Gradually, you may find that you are remembering more instances because you are 'noticing' more and interrogating the child's communicative behaviour better.

An observation chart is a way of focusing attention on a child for a short period of time and identifying the child's behaviour, your behaviour and that of the other children who interact with the child during the observation period. You need to identify a specific time period when you will notice very carefully the child's or young person's interactions, for example, a particular activity, or ten minutes in the day. You need to prepare several questions for yourself which you are going to collect information about (see Box 4.2). The example here is for an observation of a child who has difficulties using language in small group learning, and the information should show what she/he is able to do, as well as what she/he has difficulties with.

Box 4.2: Questions to guide child observation

Name of child, age, today's date

1. Is (name) attending/listening to the talk directed to her/him?
2. Does s/he turn to her/his name being called: always, sometimes, never?
3. How many times do the other children talk to her/him?
4. Some examples of what they say to her/him.
5. How many times does she/he respond?
6. Some examples of interactions.
7. How many times does she/he start to talk to someone?
8. Some examples of what she/he says.
9. How many utterances are appropriate/relevant to the situation?
10. What does she/he say that seems inappropriate/irrelevant?

There are examples of observation charts elsewhere, such as in *Teaching Talking* (by Ann Locke and Maggie Beech referred to earlier in this chapter). They show you how to log the information in a grid with the questions noted on one axis and the days and times of observation on the other axis. Thus, you have a substantial amount of data collected in an easy-to-refer-to format, which may make finding a pattern of communication behaviour easier to spot.

Tape recording. Audio tape recording of an interaction between teacher and pupil or between peers is a valuable way of collecting naturalistic spoken data (see Box 4.3). Video recording can be more difficult to set up and possibly more inhibiting for the pupils. Having tape recorders regularly and frequently on tables in the classroom soon takes the novelty away and children become more accustomed to them. They usually enjoy listening to themselves. Tape recordings can be an important teaching approach as well for some pupils with language and communication difficulties. Where a pupil registers dislike for, or becomes distressed by, taping then talk it through with the child.

Tape recorded classroom interactions can show two important features. Firstly, that teachers often do most of the talking and often at a complex and fast pace which makes it difficult for children with language difficulties to understand. Teachers hearing themselves on tape in class learn a great deal about their own use of language. Secondly, that pupils often have few opportunities to talk expansively or to talk at all. Children with language difficulties are often silent throughout the class unless particular attention and strategies are focused on that pupil.

The downside of taping classroom interaction is that it needs to be transcribed (written down) to appreciate and study what is being said, by whom and the implications. Transcription is time consuming. Fifteen minutes of tape recording takes about an hour to transcribe. It is well worth it and one transcription offers a great deal of information which colleagues will learn from too. It is helpful to discuss the transcript with someone who has had some experience in language description and analysis, such as the speech and language therapist if possible. The most important aspect of looking at these transcripts is that we see clearly that the communication difficulty lies as much with the child as it does with the person they are speaking to. With our own language we can exacerbate or support the child's communication difficulties.

Box 4.3: Tape recording activity

Make a 15 minute audio tape recording when you are teaching, and transcribe the middle five minutes. Notice your own talk time in comparison with pupil talk time.

Use the transcript to answer the questions about the language and learning environment in Boxes 4.4, 4.5, and 4.6.

You can also ask parents to do tape recordings of talk situations with the child or young person outside school, such as at bedtime, in the car, or when friends come to visit. We need to be aware that the child uses language differently across contexts for particular purposes, with variation in words, expressions, questions, and people will respond differently to the child in these contexts. Information from a variety of contexts, helps to identify which communication acts and strategies best support communication for the child with language difficulties.

Appraisal of the learning context

It is important to appraise how children with speech and language difficulties communicate in the learning context. Two key appraisal features are language and context, and there are two aspects of language to note. Firstly, there is the language for teaching, whether this is from the teacher, from peers in group learning, or from written instructions and worksheets, and secondly, there is the language of the learner in response or non-response. There are also two important features of context to note: the organisational context, such as whole class, group, pairs or individual, and then the context of the learning task, including the subject content, what the learners have to do, the kind of outcome of their learning. Language and context are interwoven: the content and nature of the task are intimately related to the vocabulary, questions and responses. Many language environments can be too complex for learners with language difficulties and successful teaching and learning is achieved by creating a balance between the demands of learning and the language capabilities and needs of the learners.

In Boxes 4.4, 4.5 and 4.6 are guidelines which may help you to appraise the aspects which influence the learning of the child with speech and language difficulties. You can apply these guidelines when observing someone else's class, or studying the audio or video recording of your own teaching session.

Box 4.4: Teacher's language

---

1. Presentation of the learning task: at the beginning of the task . . .

Was the attention called of all the learners, particularly (name of child)?

Were the aims of the learning task made clear?

Was what the learners had to do presented clearly?

Were the outcomes of the task (what each child had to produce) made clear?

Were the key words clearly presented in a way that (name) could understand?

Was a check made that (name) understood what was required of her/him?

How did (name) respond to show understanding?

How appropriate and understandable was the response?

How might the communication have been improved in this phase?

2. Communication during the task:

Does the teacher have regularly-used strategies for supporting (name)'s language?

    for example: repeating the question or instruction

    using louder, slower way of speaking

    using sign language, or mime

    using visual aids: pictures, labels, time lines

    waiting for a response

How does the teacher talk?

    one instruction at a time – with check for understanding

    several instructions at a time

    instructions matching sequence of activities

    time given for response/questions from pupils, particularly (name)

How does the teacher explain key words?

    uses written form (on the board, labels, flash cards)

    uses other words to describe them (similar, opposites, categories)

    uses other visual aids

Which if any of these strategies is noticeably more effective on (name)'s work?

What kind of communication does the activity encourage among the learners?

Box 4.5: Learner's language

1. Understanding the task:

Was (name) listening when the task was presented?

How long did (name) appear to be attending?

Did (name) show understanding of what was expected of her/him?

How? and was it understood by the teacher?

Did (name) show that she/he had difficulties understanding?

>   look puzzled
>
>   lose attention
>
>   ask for help
>
>   Some examples of what they were ....
>
>   ....

Did (name) not do the activity or do it differently from expected?

What was the teacher's response to this?

2. **Communication during the task:**

Does (name) seem aware of others as a source of help in the activity?

Does (name) wait to see what the other pupils are doing before starting?

Does (name) talk to peers in the activity?

>   some examples ....
>
>   ....

Does (name) ask for help when in difficulty?

>   teacher, assistant, peers, special friend

Does (name) use forms of communication other than talking?

>   signing or mime
>
>   writing
>
>   labels
>
>   pointing

Does (name) collaborate or not get on with peers during the activity?

>   some examples ....
>
>   ....

Box 4.6: Learning environment

1. Learning organisation for the task

Is the task organised for:

    whole class

    small group

    pairs

    individual?

Is the learning group formal or informal, in an activity corner, or open plan?

Is there a difference in (name)'s attention on the activity when

    the class noise level is high?

    there is a quiet environment?

Is time spent individually with (name) during the task?

    by whom

    for how long

Which type of learning environment does (name) do best in?

    based on evidence from   attention

                               completion of activity

                               outcome/product

                               interaction

2. Task organisation

Was the relevance of the learning task to the children and to (name):

    pointed out? understood?

Was the level of the task appropriate for the cognitive demand of (name)?

Was the level and type of contextual support appropriate for (name)?

Were the resources appropriate for task and for (name), e.g. reading, familiarity of objects?

Does (name) remember what to do in the task?

    how to start

    sequence of activities

    use of resources

    outcome/evidence of learning

Note the evidence from (name)'s behaviour to support your observation.

How could the teaching of the task organisation be improved to enhance (name)'s learning?

Summary

Appraising the language and the opportunities for interaction can give the teacher insights into the appropriateness and adequacy of the communicative strategies in teaching/learning contexts. The quality of the observation depends on the questions guiding the teacher; the more focused they are the more likely they are to identify crucial features of successful learning and communication stategies. The questions may change and develop as the teacher becomes more experienced in watching and noticing the language and learning behaviour of the pupils. Box 4.7 shows a profile of a learner with substantial communication difficulties obtained by a teacher from observation of language used for learning and social interactions.

Box 4.7: Learner's profile

Name: Trevor   **Age:** 10 years   **Period of observation:** 25–29 January 1999

- Speaks clearly.
- Engages and enjoys one-on-one talk but loses attention in group/whole class talk.
- Good at labelling, but with only one meaning per word; does not understand ambiguity.
- Difficulties in working out 'how' and 'why' questions.
- Difficulties in explaining when he has a problem.
- Often does not understand when he needs help.
- Often does not understand what he has to do in an activity, and does nothing or something different; seems naughty, willful or disobedient.
- Does not signal to others in interaction when he has not understood, or ask conversational partner for clarification.
- Understands how to behave and be polite in familiar situations but needs help to apply this knowledge to new situations; can appear rough and rude.
- Difficulties in understanding and reconstructing sequences, e.g. in completing activities, telling stories, recounting events.
- In interaction, when asked to clarify what he says, his only strategy is repetition.
- Cannot choose different words, or sentence structures.
- Does not seem to be aware of what conversational partner is likely to know or be interested in; can appear to be a 'conversational bore'.
- Has difficulty maintaining the topic of the interaction and tends to jump from topic to topic; appears to 'butterfly'.
- Does not understand puns, sarcasm, irony, idioms or any play on words; takes literal meaning; seems to lack a sense of humour.
- In discussion, has difficulty in learning a new perspective, sticks to one point of view; seems stubborn.

Possibly some of these points on their own would not indicate a communication difficulty. However, when they reoccur over several observations across a variety of learning contexts and seem to prevent new learning taking place, then taken collectively they form a profile. From this profile, it would be possible for the child's teacher to develop strategies for teaching and learning which build on the learner's strengths, such as doing more work in pairs and small groups rather than whole-class work.

Social language in the classroom

Language in the classroom and in the school not only serves learning purposes but is also used for social purposes: for example, politeness routines, such as greetings and farewells, saying please and thank you, asking permission. Language is used for negotiating, assertion and denial, rule-making and decision-making, as well as for humour and expressing emotions. Learners with language difficulties need to be taught these aspects of language use just as much as they need to be taught the language of the curriculum.

Social language is also used to praise and celebrate children's behaviour. However, judging from the findings of one study which showed that most primary school children receive nearly five times as many negative comments a day as they do positive ones, this aspect of social language used by teachers could be increased (Merrett and Wheldall 1987). Praise is particularly important for learners with language and communication difficulties. Praise is a good way of signalling specific learning success. For example, when the learner has responded well to a listening task, such as listening to the instructions for a learning task, saying 'well done, Jason, you listened all the time I was speaking', or ' well done, you remembered the two things that you have to do', is a strong reward for the learner. As we saw from the learner's profile (Box 4.7), some of the difficulties children and young people with communication difficulties have is not recognising their difficulties and when they need help. Praise is a positive indicator in helping them to develop strategies to improve their communication skills.

More importantly, language is used to organise and control pupils: for example, instructing them how to move together (e.g. to go to another lesson), prepare for a learning session, or complete (tidy away) an activity, prepare to go home, quieten the noise level, hurry up, slow down, and so on. Particular wording of these kind of instructions may need to be explicitly explained to some pupils with speech and language difficulties. For example, the meaning of 'punctual', admonitions 'that behaviour is unacceptable' and the school rules may need to be explicitly explained (Freedman and Wiig 1995).

There are examples showing how some teachers can be excessive in their use of social language when giving instructions to pupils about what to do when, where and in what sequence. The example in Box 4.8 is cited in an informative book about speech and language difficulties in school (Daines *et al.* 1996) and it is taken from a teacher in a primary school in the north of England; the extract is from the middle of a long set of instructions. As you read through this, imagine the effect on primary school children with no language difficulties and the effect on children who have difficulties.

Box 4.8: An example of teacher talk
(Adapted from Alexander 1995, p. 130, and cited in Daines *et al.* 1996)

Mr I: . . .

'The first group who are going to try the collage this afternoon is the blue group. Yellow group this afternoon are going to start with some tens and units sums. The red group are going to finish off those cards we were doing this morning, and then we're going to do some more writing about the different kinds of clothes that we're wearing . . . that we wear. If you are working in the wet area, the blue group, you've to be sensible. You've to be careful with the glue and the scissors. Don't stick one big piece of material for the whole shape of the bird: cut the material into small pieces and put different material to make up a pattern for the body of the bird. That way it looks much better when it's finished. I want to see the yellow table working each one on your own to begin with this afternoon, not doing the sum with your friend or the person sitting next to you, but doing it on your own, to see what answer you're going to get . . . Red group: when you've finished the card you were doing from this morning, then you draw the picture that's on the white sheet and leave enough space to put the words that go with the different pieces of clothing, and I will come and read them to you. So, if the blue group go quietly outside there are some pieces of paper with the shape of the bird already on them. . .'

Can you remember what the yellow group is going to do now and where? Perhaps you glanced back at the text to check that you were right! However, the children had no text to refer to and had to remember these instructions in their auditory memory. For a learner with language difficulties this would be challenging, and possibly not feasible.

Consequently, this pupil may have stopped attending and listening quite early on in the instructions when auditory memory was overloaded and she/he was no longer understanding. This learner may then have remained seated when all the other pupils were moving to their groups, or looked around and hesitatingly followed one of the groups. How might these behaviours be interpreted by the teacher?

It is worth considering how the teacher's communication might be improved to facilitate the understanding of all the children, and particularly that of the pupil with language difficulties.

Here are some simple guidelines about giving instructions to pupils, whether or not they have language difficulties:

⇨ identify the pupil or group of pupils you wish to give instructions to
⇨ get their attention by calling them by their group name, or individual names
⇨ give them their instructions in short simple sentences
⇨ make sure that the sequence of instructions matches that of the activities they will do

⇨ use important sequencing words, such as 'first', 'then', 'after', 'later'
⇨ check they have understood what to do, how and where to do it
⇨ do this for each group and task

If you suspect that some pupils have difficulty remembering instructions then consider strategies and resources in which their auditory memory can be supported. For example, write on a sheet of paper some key words corresponding to the stages and sequence of the activity. If they have difficulty reading, then draw a picture of the key words (e.g. table, material, glue, scissors, bird).

Views of the learner: self-assessment

There is concern among educational authorities and inspectorate bodies that pupils' views are rarely sought in assessment of their difficulties, and when preparing and reviewing their individual education plans (IEPs) and provision. It is still not common practice to ask pupils who have difficulties what their own views and feelings are about their difficulties, particularly children and young people with speech, language and communication difficulties. Reluctance may in part be because we anticipate that these learners will not be able to express themselves and make their views understood. Yet in the experience of teachers and others working with this group of learners they are capable of communicating their perspective, including those who have substantial communication difficulties due to physical or neurological reasons or who are within the autistic spectrum of need.

The challenge is how we seek their views. Children and young people with communication difficulties can be given the opportunity to speak or write about their feelings concerning their needs and difficulties (see Box 4.9). They may also wish to voice their views about those aspects of their education which they perceive as supporting them most effectively, as well as identifying more unhelpful aspects. Others can express themselves through art and drawing, and some through pointing to pictures suggesting particular scenarios and emotions. Moreover, we can gain a great deal of information about children's feelings through observing, asking, listening, and being sensitive to their efforts to communicate.

There are several implications from obtaining information about the views of pupils with communication difficulties. Firstly, this information can, and possibly should, influence the planning of educational programmes and provision concerning them. Secondly, there are implications for aspects of the pastoral curriculum concerning the development of self-esteem and emotional and social development. Finally, there are implications for whole-school policies about the curriculum, particularly with regard to language and literacy policies, and pastoral development of all pupils concerning understanding the issues around difference, disability and diversity. For example, policies need to be implemented which support each teacher being aware of the pupils who have communication difficulties, and knowing how best to support them in teaching and pastoral care.

Box 4.9: Activity about learner's views

Ask a child with speech and language difficulties, whom you teach, their views about their teaching, learning and achievement. You may need to consider how you will phrase the questions and how the child/young person can best respond.

Conclusions

This chapter has offered a range of procedures for collecting evidence about the speech and language of pupils whose communication is causing concern. Initial procedures should include class screening and progress through to more detailed observation and language study. Offering opportunities to pupils to talk about their learning and achievement is a crucial part of the assessment process, although often overlooked. The next chapter looks at the ways in which teachers can support pupils with speech and language difficulties in classroom learning, and offer them strategies to support learning for life.

CHAPTER 5

Managing speech and language difficulties in the classroom

This chapter looks at using language in the curriculum to support children who have speech and language difficulties to access the curriculum and achieve their learning potential. These issues are considered through curriculum planning, implementation and evaluation. Language and learning strategies are explored which support this group of learners to learn and develop language through the curriculum. Managing the wider learning environment for learners with language difficulties is also discussed.

Curriculum planning for language

Working with language in the curriculum develops teachers' awareness of language for learning, which affects their language for teaching. Teaching the curriculum with new words, familiar words with new meanings, new ways of putting words together, makes demands on learners which are additional to learning subject content. Understanding language and how it works helps teachers of children with language difficulties to plan for children's language learning. All children benefit from having their awareness of language raised.

Planning curriculum lessons

Five basic strategies can be considered which guide planning curriculum lessons (Freedman and Wiig 1995).

1. Identify the specified goals and outcomes of this aspect of the curriculum
Clarify the focus of the lesson and identify what is going to be taught: a concept, a process or a skill.

2. Differentiate and prioritise learning outcomes
Identify what is essential that **everyone** must learn, what **most** should learn, and what **some** will learn if they can. This could tie in with the three groups of language and communication skills already identified in class. Pick out the concepts, and cognitive/thinking processes, such as analysing/categorising, synthesising, evaluating, drawing inferences and problem-solving for the lesson. Concept learning can be achieved by increasing levels of sophistication from automatic

learning (rote), and the social application of rote learning to solve a problem, through to systematic application of a body of knowledge to solve a problem, and ability to generalise knowledge to show an awareness of an abstract concept. For example, developing concepts for coin values across the different levels.

3. Need for a pre-teaching session

Determine the need for a session to identify and teach pre-concepts, skills and core vocabulary. Check out assumptions of the pupils' prior knowledge.

4. Modifications for learners with speech and language needs

In planning the lesson, develop options which include learning for pupils who do not have the pre-concepts, core vocabulary, key words or new meanings. Identify pupils with language needs and ensure that everyone can learn in the lesson. Consider collaborative group study, guided questioning, scaffolding, mediation, as well as stimulating interaction. Include activities which develop categorisation and defining skills. Develop strategies for semantic networking, 'meaning webs' for core vocabulary and key words. Consider including activities which facilitate learners to generalise and integrate the new learning and language into the 'real world'.

5. Evaluation

Try to assess your own teaching: what did I really teach the pupils? Consider ways you could evaluate this. Reflect on whether every pupil had equal access to the learning opportunities in the lesson. Consider how you can evaluate what each student has learnt and the range of learning in this lesson.

Planning for language in the lesson: Rich Scripting

While teachers cannot plan or predict all the language which may emerge in the classroom talk of a lesson, there are important steps which they can take to prepare and anticipate the language for learning to support all children and in particular those with additional language difficulties. Many teachers are familiar with 'Rich Scripting' which is an approach to targeting words and phrases which are central to the learning aims of a topic (McWilliam 1998). If you are interested in this approach Norah McWilliam's book is recommended: *What's in a Word: Vocabulary Development in Multilingual Classrooms* (see References section).

Language demands and opportunities

When planning for language, two important aspects need to be considered which can guide teachers.

⇨ language demands on the pupil: Which vocabulary items (words and phrases) do pupils have to understand and use if they are to participate successfully in learning?

⇨ opportunities to learn new language for the pupil: How can attention to key words in this activity/lesson extend the vocabulary of pupils generally, and develop and consolidate vocabulary for pupils with speech and language difficulties?

Identifying key words

Identifying 'key words' in the lesson topic is essential. Children who have difficulties learning key words will not understand or learn the concepts being taught unless they are explicitly explained and explored. They need more support in learning key words than their peers. Key words are technical terminology used to teach content, as well as key question words and phrases. They can be new words, or familiar words with new, technical meanings. Geography offers some examples: the technical word 'gradient' is crucial to learning how we measure the steepness of hills. There are non-technical words which have technical meanings, such as 'key', which geographically means the list of explanations for the map symbols, usually found in a corner of the map. An example of a key question is one which is central to the learning of the topic: If the time in ...... is ......, what is the time in......? A question like: What will happen next? has no key vocabulary items and is hard for children with language difficulties. Easier to undestand is: What will the ...... do next?

Planning language opportunities

To develop children's understanding of word-meaning, the lesson needs to draw attention to appropriate ways of exploring networks of meaning around key words. For example: definitions, synonyms, opposites, linking with experience, similies, grammatical functions, roots and affixes, phrases and sayings. Opportunities can be planned for pupils to show their curiosity about language by asking each other, using dictionaries and flash cards – taking note that children with language difficulties may need differentiated tasks and to work at their own pace. Opportunities to develop awareness of words at other levels of language, such as phonological awareness and through writing (such as on flash cards or on computer). Planning these opportunities encourages teachers to develop their own awareness of word-meanings and their use in language.

Implementation

Implementing language planning effectively with children who have speech and language difficulties requires strategies for *listening, understanding, expression* and *organisational* skills. For example, reinforcing the classroom code for 'listening' behaviour, 'signposting' (indicating) when class/children need to listen carefully to information, and calling children by their name, all improve attention and listening.

Effective understanding is helped by presentation of the aims and content of the lesson, and other good teaching practices. For children with language difficulties, teachers need to use simple, short sentences to explain and give instructions, be prepared to repeat explanations, questions and instructions when necessary, and check that the child has understood. They should also encourage children to say when they have not understood instructions, and this may mean teaching them a script, such as: 'I don't understand you, please say it again.' Teachers should avoid irony and sarcasm because most children dislike it and learners who have pragmatic language difficulties are likely to misunderstand it. 'Quick fire' question–response type interactions do not give pupils with language processing difficulties sufficient time to respond. Multiple meanings of key words, particularly literal and abstract meanings, need to be explicitly explained, building from the primary meaning of the word.

Strategies for implementing effective *expressive language* include allowing more processing time with children who have language difficulties, repairing and modelling appropriate or target words and responses, and selecting appropriate questioning style, (closed, open) for the learning purpose.

Effective organisational skills are developed through sequences and organisational tasks, such as drawing attention to the sequence of events in stories, routines, and using pictures of the events in the learning task, and when reporting or re-telling the sequence of events. In teacher talk organisational skills are improved by identifying and drawing the child's attention to important sequence words, such as 'first, last, next, then, because, before, after, later'. Explicit discussion helps the child to plan and verbalise organising the sequence before executing it. These skills are often best done in small groups and individual teaching.

Differentiation

There are two important aspects to differentiating learning around language; firstly, differentiating level and extent of language development, and secondly, differentiating between *language* learning and *content* learning.

Planning a range of opportunities to explore and develop language for learning offers possibilities for differentiated teaching and learning in a mainstream class. Implementing these opportunities can be done at small group level, where the groups have been carefully organised by the teacher. Most groups are able to develop and extend the language learning opportunities to the maximum, extending the range of opportunities prepared by the teacher. Groups of children with language difficulties may need teacher or adult support to develop the basic key word language meanings and extend to some of the less frequent meanings and usages.

Children need to have the language for learning before they have the content for learning. This is particularly so with children who have difficulties learning through language. Part of the differentiation between language and content is seen in the implementation strategies just discussed. Spending time at the beginning of the session on activities which introduce and explore the language to be used in the content learning is an effective strategy. In some cases it may mean dedicating a whole session to exploring the language for learning. Some teachers may feel anxious about dedicating so much time to a language preparation lesson, thinking that it is taking time away from the more important aspect of learning content. It is worthwhile monitoring and reflecting on the way pupils in the class respond to these approaches. Evaluating the outcome of different approaches to language learning and content learning can enhance teaching.

In summary, effective **learning of language** depends on:

- the teacher's awareness of the linguistic demands of the learning task;
- management of her/his own language;
- management of the pupil's attention and understanding of the language;

and effective **learning of content** depends on:

- effective learning of language linked with the content;
- teacher's awareness of the cognitive demands of the learning task;
- management of the pupil's attention and understanding of the learning content.

Supporting study and organisational skills

Many learners with speech and language difficulties need to be taught strategies to support their study skills and organisation of learning. These strategies can be introduced to children in primary school and developed and consolidated in secondary schools. Further strategies may need to be developed for examination study skills; strategies that develop skills in using resources, and management of learning, improve memorising and recall. Also, there may be learners who have literacy difficulties who may benefit from these strategies.

Using resources
This group of learners need to be explicitly taught how to use dictionaries, thesauri and computer word processing functions. In textbooks the purpose and location of the list of contents and the index, titles of chapters, headings and subheadings need to be explained. Tape recorders may be used to tape lessons which have talk and discussion which are too demanding on auditory processing for some learners with language and/or literacy difficulties. There needs to be a supply of tapes, recorders and batteries in the classroom since many of these learners will also lack the organisational abilities to bring these resources to school.

Management of learning
Building strategies for learning through visual skills is helpful for many learners with speech and language difficulties (Bray 1995). Encouraging them to draw

semantic maps of what they have understood of the teacher's presentation or what they have read helps understanding and learning. Other learners may prefer setting down the ideas in a linear outline. Prepared questions help to focus attention on key information when listening or reading. At a later stage they can make up their own questions to help their comprehension and memory of the talk or text. Learning and recall are also helped by framing the information into mnemonics. Teachers will need to do this initially with pupils who have language difficulties but with practise pupils may learn to create their own mnemonics.

Explicit teaching about note-taking helps to prevent learners with language difficulties from becoming distracted after reading a few pages. For example, the student can divide the page into two columns, and write full notes on one side and the key words on the other. They can leave spaces between the main ideas to show up the ideas more clearly and also this allows more detail to be added in later. Furthermore, they should only write for a short time, such as three to five minutes because of the demands. They can monitor the amount and quality they write. They can write a paragraph about what they have read/heard, draw a sketch, a semantic map of the key ideas, or brainstorm the ideas.

Teachers and other staff can use helpful strategies. Support staff can also take notes as a model for the pupil and to offer for comparison later. During presentations, teachers can give verbal clues, such as: 'this is important', 'three important reasons', 'underline this in your notes', 'make a new heading'.

This group of pupils also need to be taught how to read charts, diagrams, graphs and other visual displays of information. Comprehension of reading can be improved by teaching strategies for using context clues, such as 'cloze' techniques, and drawing on their own experience and background knowledge about the reading material.

This group of learners can gain a great deal from talking about the strategies they prefer and sharing strategies which they have developed for themselves to help their learning, understanding and recall.

Managing the learning environment

Classroom organisation

The physical environment for the context for learning and language is as important as the structured opportunites to learn language. The classroom environment should be conducive to learning for all learners and supportive of the needs of individuals. It needs to provide a context where learners feel secure, confident and willing to take risks in order to explore and investigate knowledge. The physical environment is particularly significant for learners with communication difficulties where the type of resources, access to them and access to teacher and peers is an essential part of the support for their learning and communication.

Size of the room

A large mainstream classroom can physically be intimidating for some children with communication difficulties. It may also be difficult for them to hear and attend when people speak from different parts of the room. Open plan classrooms are particularly challenging. Most children find it difficult to attend or listen effectively in noisy, reverberant conditions. While it may be easier to establish an atmosphere of reassurance and confidence in a small class group in a small classroom, teachers need to establish a similar atmosphere with a large class in a larger room.

Making a quiet place

Whatever size the classroom it is important for all phases of teaching pupils with communication difficulties to have a quiet part of the room. In nursery and infant school it may be a corner with restful non-talk activities, and in the junior and secondary classroom it may be a corner of the class with easy chairs. The quiet corner is a physical place where children can sit quietly and re-focus; they may also choose to read, or look at books, or perhaps chat quietly to a friend. More active learning and talking happens elsewhere in the class. Learners with language difficulties can become very tired with the effort taken to attend, listen and respond to classroom learning. Having a quiet time for a few minutes during a lesson can give them the opportunity to replenish. Children, particularly those with language difficulties, should be encouraged to take short breaks. However, children should not be sent to the quiet area, otherwise it may be confused in children's minds with exclusion and punishment.

Self-organisation

Many children with speech and language difficulties have organisational needs. They find it difficult to organise themselves: their clothes may appear dishevelled, they may forget the books they need as well as having difficulties organising themselves to complete an activity. It is crucial to their learning that they are encouraged to develop strategies to organise themselves. One simple strategy is having the child keep her/his belongings consistently together in the same place, for example, a tray, a desk, a locker, a kit bag. Many primary schools do this for all children, but it may be more difficult logistically to organise in secondary school. Keeping classroom equipment consistently in the same place helps this group of learners although again this may be difficult to organise in secondary schools. Drawing maps of locations can help organise this group of learners: a map of the school, classroom, home, their desk, their school bag. Through them they can learn to locate themselves and their belongings.

Organising time: familiar routine

A familiar routine to the school day is supportive to all children and particularly to those with organisational and language difficulties. The advantages are that the children develop security and reassurance in knowing the order of the day which may help them to feel less anxious and confused. However, over-familiar routines and regimentation may make the children behave like automatons, or become bored and disinterested. Encouraging the pupils to develop strategies, such as looking at the timetable, are helpful. Teaching children to read and interpret the weekly timetable is a valuable life skill. For primary school aged children with organisational and language difficulties, it may be necessary to develop a simple timetable based on a few important activities each day throughout the week.

Young children and those with speech and language difficulties, find the idea of 'days' difficult to understand, while the notion of 'sleeps' is much easier to grasp. Introducing the idea of a week can be done by talking about the number of sleeps we have between now and the same time next week. This idea is supported by drawing ' a bed' to mean 'a sleep'. Interspersed between the sleeps/beds are the key activities in the child's school life: music on Monday (draw a recorder), PE on Tuesday (pumps); painting on Wednesday (painting overall), swimming on Thursday (costume and towel) and assembly on Friday (prizes). Important events, such as Harvest Festival, birthdays, parents evenings, can be added on for the particular week. It is possible to develop a wall frieze or a diary for the particular child, with the weeks in the term. The diary (e.g. an exercise book) can pass between home and school, where parents can develop weekly cycles for important home and family events for the child.

There is an important point of differentiation concerning when and how to introduce written words into the diary. To include too much visual stimulation early on in the diary would be counter-productive. Many children with language difficulties need to be taught to build up their skills in understanding visual stimuli as well as auditory stimuli, because many have difficulties making sense of, and using, any kind of symbol. For the nursery and infant learner with language difficulties it is advisable to introduce the diary and week cycle through pictures only. When the idea of the passage of time is developing through a cycle of sleeps, then more complex visual stimuli, such as the written word, can be introduced.

Conclusions

This chapter has discussed approaches to curriculum planning which focus on language. They have developed strategies for identifying the language demands in the curriculum and opportunities for meeting those demands. Implementation of the curriculum has been discussed in the context of differentiation for the needs of pupils with speech and language needs. The need to support organisation skills in this group of learners has been discussed in terms of study skills for older learners and strategies for organising and managing learning and the environment. Teachers cannot work in isolation with learners with speech and language needs. They require resources and the expertise of other professionals. They also need to work with parents. Schools need to consider a whole-school approach to supporting this group of learners, their teachers and their parents and families.

CHAPTER 6

Whole-school approach to communication needs

A whole-school approach to identifying and supporting the education of learners who have speech, language and communication difficulties has many advantages to teachers and to pupils.

An explicit commitment to include all pupils and staff with reference to difference, disability and diversity is needed in school mission statements. Schools need to demonstrate this commitment by developing an ethos and culture which is educationally inclusive. Educational inclusion is not simply a geographical phenomenon, where a variety of learners come together in the same buildings to study the same curriculum. Inclusive education is a teaching and learning process. It needs to be worked towards through policy development and implementation. Policies need to identify and support the curriculum and pastoral needs of individual learners and groups of pupils. They also need to support teachers to do this. The following are suggestions about how this might be carried out, with particular reference to learners with speech, language and communication difficulties.

Involvement of head teacher and senior management

When head teachers and senior management are involved in the development, integration and implementation of language policies in schools those policies are more likely to be effective. The SENCO would also need to be included when there is integration of language policies and those for pupils with special educational needs and their individual education plans (IEPs).

Integrated language and literacy policies with IEPs

Inspectorate bodies have reported that schools which have integrated whole-school policies on language and literacy are likely to have better achievement in this area than schools which do not. Furthermore, these bodies are concerned where IEPs for pupils are not linked to school language and literacy policies. In the case of children and young people with speech, language and literacy difficulties, it is all the more important for their education to have planning and provision for their needs closely related to the school's language and literacy policies and their implementation.

Policies about disseminating information

Schools have policies which ensure that staff are informed about pupils who have IEPs and the nature of their difficulty. It is equally important that schools consider policies whereby information from teachers can inform the IEPs. Inspectorate bodies are concerned that liaison should improve between primary and secondary schools over pupils who have IEPs. For example, throughout this book ways have been discussed in which teachers can obtain a great deal of information about teaching and learning with pupils who have speech and language difficulties. Schools could develop policies concerning the way in which this kind of information can be disseminated between class teachers and SENCOs.

Disseminating good practice

Reports from inspecting bodies have also observed that good practice in the area of language and communication is patchy, mainly because good practice is often not disseminated, even within the same school. Schools could consider policies which set up mechanisms and strategies for identifying and disseminating good practice with pupils who have language and communication needs. Moreover, they could develop policies to support teachers to develop classroom practices which take account of the IEPs and impact on the learning of pupils who have language and communication needs. Strategies might include meetings where planning and teaching activities are shared, as well as carrying out team teaching between class teachers and SENCOs, language or learning support teachers, outreach teachers and speech and language therapists.

Joint professional development

Schools may also need to consider policies which develop opportunities for shared professional development and a body of shared knowledge and skills about pupils with language and communication needs across a range of staff groups: teachers, assistants, playground and dinner staff. If members of staff are in contact with pupils who have speech, language and communication difficulties, it is important that they know how these pupils are likely to communicate with them, and what and how they are likely to understand communication to them. The implications of breakdowns in communication could be serious. Schools may wish to develop joint training sessions to include all school pupils, where it is necessary to develop sign language skills for some pupils' communication and learning needs.

Important others

This section looks at the important others, besides the classroom teacher, who are involved with learners who have speech and language difficulties, in the classroom, in the wider environment of the school, and beyond.

Consider Box 6.1. Are you surprised at how many names of people you have written down around the child? Some of these people you may know very well and others not at all because they are outside the school. Alternatively, did you have difficulty knowing who else is involved? Who could you ask for this information? Why do you need to know?

Box 6.1: Activity about important others for the pupil with speech and language difficulties

Think of a learner in your classroom who has speech and language difficulties. Now take a piece of paper and in the middle draw a figure to represent the child and around the figure write the names of all the people who you know, or think, are involved with this child.

Teachers most often identify the following people who are involved with children with speech and language difficulties:

In the classroom:
- classroom assistants
- other subject teachers
- form teacher
- learning and/or language support assistants

In the wider school:
- the SENCO
- dinner ladies
- bus guide, bus driver or taxi driver

Outside school:
- education psychologist
- speech and language therapist
- physiotherapist and occupational therapist
- social services
- medical: GP, health visitor, audiologist, paediatrician, ENT consultant

Home:
- parents
- family

Some of these people will be more involved with supporting the teacher than others. In the case you have in mind, who are they?

Teacher colleagues
The class teacher has most contact with teacher colleagues through staff meetings, departmental meetings and tutors' meetings. These meetings are opportunities to discuss with colleagues how they are approaching and implementing the IEPs for learners who have speech and language difficulties as well as for learners with other difficulties. Their perspective is influenced by their perception of the ability which learners with speech and language difficulties have towards their subject area and the curriculum they are offering.

Learning and/or language support assistants
Learning and/or language support assistants (LSAs) are allocated to learners whose statement of special need requires additional support in order for the learner to successfully access the curriculum. They are usually peripatetic who support learners individually in a cluster of schools. However, in many cases there is insufficient joint planning between them and class teachers. Consequently, LSAs may not be as prepared for the lesson as they could be, in which they are to support the learner. They have to rely on quick thinking to present the learning task in a way accessible to the learner, or present a different task – which they have prepared and which they know the learner can manage.

Special Educational Needs Coordinator

The school's designated member of staff for learners with special needs, the Special Educational Needs Coordinator (SENCO), is likely to know the background and the other people, both professional and family, involved with the child. There are often many people, such as educationists, medical, family and friends, who are involved in supporting the child's needs. It is important to know about them for three main reasons:

(i)   they are part of the child's life and experiences and are important to her/him;
(ii) the child may need to leave class and miss teaching/learning to keep appointments to visit some of these people;
(iii) their knowledge and experience about the child can help the teacher to support the child's language and learning more effectively in a variety of ways.

Teachers also work with professionals who are regarded as specialists in aspects of special needs and speech and language difficulties. They are often closely involved with the initial identification and assessment in the process of exploring the need to draw up a statement of a child's learning needs, and then in the management of their language and learning support.

Educational psychologists (EPs) are teachers who have professional qualifications in educational psychology. They are mainly responsible for the identification, assessment and management of learners with special educational needs. They play a central part in the statementing procedure for these learners. They usually work with teachers and SENCOs to develop IEPs for learners with difficulties.

Speech and language therapists have a degree in speech and language pathology and therapy and are usually employed by the National Health Service and often work in clinics, although some are employed by education to work directly in schools. They are concerned with the identification, assessment and management of difficulties in speech, language and communication of learners. They contribute to the statementing procedure and are involved in developing IEPs with the teacher and SENCO for learners with language difficulties. Often speech and language therapists work with these learners on an individual basis by withdrawing them from the class to be seen by the speech and language therapist in the clinic.

Other professionals are often less involved with the class teacher in the early stages of identification, and may be more involved during and after the statementing procedure, in drawing up IEPs. They include the following.

Physiotherapists have a degree in physiotherapy and work with children who have muscular difficulties affecting movement and coordination. Often language and communication difficulties is only one aspect of this group of learners' concerns. Physios may be employed by health or education and as well as working directly with children advise other practitioners involved.

Occupational therapists (OTs) have a degree in occupational therapy and work with children and young people who have difficulties developing their skills for everyday living. They may also be involved with learners with communication difficulties to develop organisational and perceptual skills. They work directly with learners and also advise on aids and equipment which support them at school and at home.

There are others in the health sector who are more involved in diagnosis and monitoring the difficulty than in the child's learning. However, their knowledge about the child has important implications for teaching and learning.

Audiologists have a degree in hearing sciences, and measure and monitor the hearing of children whose hearing causes concern. All children on entering school have their hearing screened to identify any gross difficulties. Many younger children with speech and language difficulties have some difficulties in hearing. It may be due to 'glue ear' which is caused by persistent colds and gives rise to fluctuating hearing, or it may be due to a more permanent damage to the ear. However, children with speech and language difficulties may have no physical or organic difficulty with their hearing but they may be unable to *perceive* sound, that is make sense of sounds and speech, and thus function as if they are deaf. There are only a few children with this kind of difficulty and they usually do not develop much spoken language (Byers Brown and Edwards 1989). The information from the audiologist about a learner's hearing has important implications for the class teacher. Fluctuating hearing will cause the learner's attention and performance to vary, and may also affect behaviour in class.

Some children with persistent 'glue ear', tonsillitis or other recurrent infections in the throat and nose may be referred to the **Ear, Nose and Throat (ENT) consultant**. Simple surgical interventions, such as fitting grommets (tiny valves) into the ear drum, 'cure' 'glue ear'. This simple procedure was introduced in the mid 1960s and was responsible for a substantial drop in children being identified with learning difficulties due to hearing impairment.

Other medical consultants, such as **paediatricians**, are involved with younger children who have severe difficulties which include speech and language difficulties, for example children who are over-active, have epilepsy, or physical and coordination difficulties. They may prescribe drugs which, while improving some of the child's difficulties, may have a counter affect on learning and communication, such as sedating the individual to a more passive and less responsive state.

GPs are concerned with children's overall general health and they would refer children to medical consultants. The health, well-being and development of children under five years of age is the concern of **health visitors**, who are nurses with further qualifications.

It remains difficult for classroom teachers to obtain information directly from health professionals involved with learners in their class. The SENCO in the school is the most likely source of information for teachers.

A team approach for professionals is crucial, because it can offer cohesive and coherent support to children and families. Central to such a team are the parents, teachers and therapists working with children with language and communication needs.

Working together

Box 6.2: Working with others

As a teacher involved with learners who have speech and language difficulties you need to decide who in the list of professionals you most need to develop a working relationship with in order for you to successfully support this group of learners.

The most likely professionals are the speech and language therapist, the speech and language therapy assistant and the language support teacher. Where it is important to work more closely with the speech and language therapy service, it is advisable to discuss the matter with the SENCO to decide how best to organise this.

Developing working relationships is dependent on a number of factors:

(i)   what the purpose is;
(ii) what you each aim to achieve;
(iii) how you each see your role;
(iv) how available you both are to work together;
(v)   where you both could work together.

Two ways of working with others are discussed here: liaison, and collaboration.

Liaison

When you liaise with a colleague or parent about a child, it usually involves regular but not necessarily frequent contact where you may let each other know what you are doing and maybe ask for advice about moving forward. When speech and language therapists are involved with learners in your class, you need to be in liaison with them. You may do this by arranging through the SENCO:

(a)   to meet and talk with them about specific children in your class, when they visit your school;
(b)   to telephone them about a specific child's communication difficulty.

You can arrange that regular liaison is maintained for as long as it is needed.

Referral and the Code of Practice (CoP)

In cases where the speech and language therapist is not involved, your school, through the SENCO, may be the referring agency, that is, the first to let the speech and language therapy service know that a particular child has a communication difficulty.

The procedures and circumstances for involving speech and language therapists in schools in England and Wales are clearly set out in the *Code of Practice for Identification and Assessment of Children with Special Educational Needs* (DfEE

1994). Therapists become involved when children have not progressed sufficiently through IEPs and communication difficulties are still giving cause for concern to teachers and the SENCO. This is at Stage 3 of the CoP. The demand for speech and language therapy is usually much more than the service can provide and it may be a while before the child is seen by a therapist. After the initial interview with the child and the family, a decision is reached about whether the child's identified needs are sufficiently substantial to require speech and language therapy intervention.

Collaboration

Collaborating over learners who have speech and language difficulties is working together with one or others so that you are sharing work between you. It is a much closer professional relationship than liaison. It usually requires regular and frequent contact to discuss in some detail how you are sharing the work being done with the learners. People who are likely to want to collaborate over learners who have speech and language difficulties are class teachers with parents and speech and language therapists.

Collaborating with parents and families

There is an increasing importance being placed on the need to collaborate with parents since the family environment affects children's language and communication skills as much as the school.

Parents' expectation of teachers and schools are often influenced by their own experiences as pupils and they vary from positive to negative. Their perception of their child's speech and language may be different from the teacher's. They may not perceive any difficulty, or a difficulty which is less severe, or a difficulty of a different nature, from that noticed by the teachers. For example, parents may be concerned that their child is not reading and not concerned that she/he has difficulty remembering new vocabulary.

Many speech and language difficulties have been found to run in families. Some may be genetic and more common in the males in the family. It is possible that there are other members of the child's family, possibly one of the parents, who have difficulties similar to that of the child's. Teachers need to be mindful of the implications of this possibility when discussing the child's difficulties. Working in collaboration with a specialist language support teacher or a speech and language therapist is helpful in these circumstances.

Parents may have had contact previously with speech and language services and have views about the service and its benefits for their child. These may include a belief that a model based on one-to-one interaction between the therapist and their child in a quiet place withdrawn from the classroom, is the ideal. Alternatives, such as support from a language support assistant in the classroom may be difficult for them to accept. They may see this kind of help as a 'watering down' of speech and language support and be less willing to collaborate with the teachers and school.

Parents would need to be persuaded of the benefits of an inclusive approach to their child's needs which would be most effectively done through a collaborative approach by teachers and therapists. Teachers and therapists need to convince parents of the rationale for inclusion and to explain to them the manner in which support will be realised.

Parents who have been involved with other professionals for their child's sake, may be more accustomed to understanding and using medical terms to describe the difficulty. Taking a collaborative approach, teachers and therapists need to explain to parents the relationship between the specific medical-type diagnostic labels used for the communication difficulty and the curriculum-based educational approach to intervention and support for the child's language and learning needs. For example, a child's difficulty may be described by the clinical label 'dyspraxia' which means a cluster of difficulties involving motor coordination in speech and other movements and possibly more widespread organisational difficulties. Educationally, this translates into developing strategies with the child to: support activities which require verbal responses and interaction to learning tasks, develop reading, spelling and writing skills, as well as develop sequencing and organisational abilities to manage curriculum learning. While these strategies may be developed in the classroom, parents need to be trained and supported in using and establishing them at home and in other non-school contexts.

There are a variety of ways which teachers and parents can collaborate for children who have special needs including communication difficulties:

- furnishing information about their child, such as medical details;
- collaborating with home–school programmes, such as reading or behaviour;
- helping as classroom aides and supporting other parents;
- communicating about their child through home–school diaries, handbooks, telephone, (schools are more likely to use them proactively and parents to respond);
- parent–teacher evenings;
- home visits;
- parent workshops.

Collaborating with speech and language therapists

Most speech and language therapists are employed by health trusts while teachers are employed by education authorities. Several important obstacles to collaborative practice arise from this, concerning perspectives towards children with speech and language difficulties and others concern the structures and practices of the two services. Teachers and therapists agree that when certain organisational changes take place it is easier to develop and establish collaborative practices. For example, in place of ad hoc encounters in the corridor, teachers and therapists collaborate better when there is a programmmed time to meet to discuss and plan support for children with speech and language difficulties, and a designated room for this meeting. There are increasing numbers of examples of collaboration practice based on formalised arrangements through the schools' and therapy services' development plans. Collaboration across services may also need support from higher levels of management.

Training for teachers and speech and language therapists

Joint in-service and professional development has been identified as important for successful collaboration. Teachers and therapists who had shared in-service training sessions and professional development courses appreciated their differing professional perspectives, responsibilities and work practices, as well as being able to develop shared perspectives and work practices. At a local level, shared training sessions can be organised between the speech and language therapy service and the education authority. Regional and national professional development courses may be available for both therapists and teachers. The important outcome of professional development courses is that they facilitate teachers and therapists collaborating to support learners with speech, language and communication difficulties to learn both in school and beyond.

If you would like to read more about this aspect, the following book is recommended:

McCartney, E. (ed.) (1999) *Speech/Language Therapists and Teachers Working Together: A Systems Approach to Collaboration.* London: Whurr.

Conclusion

The final chapter in the book has focused on the team of people, professionals and parents, who are usually involved in supporting children with speech and language difficulties. School policies can go a long way to supporting class teachers in supplying resources, allowing time for liaison and collaborative work with colleagues and parents, and in creating an ethos in the school which promotes diversity and difference. Opportunities to share joint professional development courses can be created by good local practice and organisation. One of the outcomes is that teachers and other professionals develop shared concepts of professional roles and expertise which are more effective in supporting the language and learning of pupils who have speech and language difficulties.

Whole-class observation checklist

Class Year: .... Date: .... Completed by: ....

Communication behaviour	Names of pupils
Listening behaviour	
Often has difficulties attending in whole-class activities	
Engages in one-to-one talk	
Instructions usually need to be repeated	
Often does not understand what she/he has to do	
Difficulty understanding some questions	
Expressive language	
Speech sounds are unclear	
Hesitates, repeats, stammers	
Telegraphic/short utterances	
Rarely starts a conversation	
Unexpected responses to questions	
Social behaviour	
Unusual interaction with peers and adults	
Difficulties in cooperating with others	
Organisational difficulties	
Coordination difficulties/clumsiness	
Aggressive to others/temper tantrums	

The AFASIC checklists: 4–5 years, 6–10 years

Example of the checklist for 4–5-year-olds

Language content

Attention and comprehension   tick if yes

(a) Able to attend to stimuli from two different sources (completing a jigsaw, listening to the tescher) ☐

(b) Listens attentively to a simple story ('The Three Little Pigs') ☐

(c) Able to follow stories unaccompanied by pictures ☐

(d) Able to follow simple instructions ('Pick up the book and take it to the other room') ☐

(e) Understands the spatial concepts 'in', 'on', 'under' ☐

(f) Understands words relating to time (yesterday, tomorrow, this afternoon) ☐

(g) Understands emotion words (happy, sad, angry) ☐

(h) Able to classify objects into categories (types of fruit or animal) ☐

Subtotal ——————

Vocabulary and expressive language

(a) Has wide vocabulary of basic words ☐

(b) Is able to name shapes (square, circle, triangle) ☐

(c) Is able to name sizes (big, small, tall, short) ☐

(d) Uses comparatives (bigger, smaller, taller, shorter) ☐

(e) Uses adverbs (quickly, slowly, loudly, quietly) ☐

(f) Uses appropriate pronouns (I, me, my, mine, you, yours, your) ☐

(g) Is able to summarise the content of stories ☐

(h) Is able to describe a sequence of events ('They had a bath and then went to bed') ☐

Subtotal ——————
Total for this section ——————

Example of the checklist for 6–10-year-olds

Errors in sound

tick if yes

(a) Omits the beginnings and endings of words ('pretending' becomes 'tending') ☐

(b) Reduces multisyllabic words ('potato' becomes 'tato') ☐

(c) Speaks less intelligibly when excited ☐

(d) Speaks less intelligibly when attempting a lengthy utterance ☐

(e) Shows persistent confusion between voiced and unvoiced sounds (p/b, f/v ,t/d, k/g) ☐

Total for this section ———

Communication

(a) Has delayed understanding of question words (what, who) ☐

(b) Does not follow instructions without prompting ☐

(c) Offers limited verbal comments on own activities ☐

(d) Shows unexpected responses to questions ☐

(e) Uses inappropriate intonation and volume when speaking ☐

Total for this section ———

Play and recreation

(a) Has difficulty following a story without many visual cues ☐

(b) Has no play involving sounds, rhymes or words ☐

(c) Is slow to learn rules of group games and positions in sports ☐

(d) Enjoys the visual content of television programmes but finds it hard to follow stories and plots ☐

(e) Humour tends towards visual and slapstick with poor appreciation of verbal jokes and puns ☐

Total for this section ———

References

Andersen-Wood, L. and Smith, B. R. (1997) *Working with Pragmatics*, 40–41. Bicester: Winslow Press.

Baumgaertel, A. (2000) 'Attention Deficit Disorder', in Law, J. (eds) *Communication Difficulties in Childhood*. Oxford: Radcliffe Medical Press.

Bloom, L. and Lahey, M. (eds) (1978) *Language Development and Language Disorders*. New York: Wiley.

Boehm, A. E. (1986) *Boehm Test of Basic Concepts – Revised (Boehm-R)*. London: The Psychological Corporation/Harcourt Brace.

Bray, C. (1995) Developing study, organisation and management strategies for adolescents with language disabilities', *Seminars in Speech and Language* **16**(1), 65–84.

Brown, R. (1973) *A First Language: The Early Stages*. Cambridge, Mass.: Harvard University Press.

Byers Brown, B. and Edwards, M. (1989) *Developmental Disorders of Language*. London: Whurr.

Crystal, D. (1987) 'Towards a "bucket" theory of language disability: taking account of interaction between linguistic levels', *Clinical Linguistics and Phonetics* **1**(1),7–22.

Daines, B. *et al.* (1996) *Spotlight on Special Educational Needs: Speech and Language Difficulties*. Stoke: NASEN, in association with AFASIC.

Department for Education and Employment (DfEE) (1994) *Code of Practice for Identification and Assessment of Children with Special Educational Needs*. London: HMSO.

Dewart, H. and Summers, S. (1995) *The Pragmatics Profile of Everyday Communication Skills in School Aged Children*. Windsor: NFER-Nelson.

Dockrell, J. and Lindsay, G. (1998) 'The ways in which speech and language difficulties impact on children's access to the curriculum', *Child Language Teaching and Therapy*, **14**(2), 117–33.

Freedman, E. and Wiig, E. (1995) 'Classroom management and instruction for adolescents with language disabilities', *Seminars in Speech and Language* **16**(1) 46–64.

Grauberg, E. (1999) *Early Mathematics and Language Difficulties*. London: Whurr.

Hughes, M. and Westgate, D. (1997) 'Assistants as talk-partners in early-years classrooms: some issues of support and development', *Educational Review*, **49**(1), 5–12.

Hughes, M. and Westgate, D. (1998) 'Possible enabling strategies in teacher-led talk with young pupils', *Language and Education* **12**(3), 174–91.

I CAN (1999) *Annual Review*. Available from I CAN Central Office, 4 Dyer's Buildings, Holborn, London EC1N 2QP. I CAN is the national educational charity for children with speech and language difficulties.

Law, J. (2000a) 'Children's communication: development and difficulties', in Law, J. *et al.* (eds) *Communications Difficulties in Childhood*. Oxford: Radcliffe Medical Press.

Law, J. *et al.* (eds) (200b) *Communication Difficulties in Childhood*. Oxford: Radcliffe Medical Press.

Lock, J. (1993) *The Child's Path to Spoken Language*. Cambridge, Mass.: Harvard University Press.

Locke, A. and Beech, M. (1991) *Teaching Talking: A Screening and Intervention Programme for Children with Speech and Language Difficulties*. Windsor: NFER-Nelson.

Lumb and Lumb (1987) *Early Mathematics Diagnostic Kit*.

McWilliam, N. (1998) *What's in a Word: Vocabulary Development in Multilingual Classrooms*. Stoke: Trentham Books.

Merrett, F. and Wheldall, K. (1987) 'Natural rates of teacher approval and disapproval in British primary and middle school classrooms', *British Journal of Educational Psychology* **57**(1), 95–103.

Perera, K. (1986) 'Language acquisition and writing', in Fletcher, P. and Garman, M. (eds) *Language Acquisition*, 2nd edn. Cambridge: Cambridge University Press.

Portwood, M. (1999) *Understanding Developmental Dyspraxia*. London: David Fulton Publishers.

Rapin, I. (1996) 'Developmental language disorders: a clinical update', *Journal of Child Pyscology and Psychiatry* **37**(6), 643–55.

Sinclair, J. (ed.) (1987) *Collins Cobuild English Language Dictionary*. London: Collins.

Thorley, G. (2000) 'Behavioural difficulties', in Law, J. *et al.* (eds) *Communication Difficulties in Childhood* Oxford: Radcliffe Medical Press.

Index